Learning Apache Thrift

Make applications communicate using Apache Thrift

Krzysztof Rakowski

PUBLISHING

BIRMINGHAM - MUMBAI

Learning Apache Thrift

First published: December 2015

Production reference: 1181215

Published by Packt Publishing Ltd.
Livery Place
35 Livery Street
Birmingham B3 2PB, UK.

ISBN 978-1-78588-274-6

www.packtpub.com

Credits

Author
Krzysztof Rakowski

Reviewer
Faisal Rahman

Commissioning Editor
Dipika Gaonkar

Acquisition Editor
Rahul Nair

Content Development Editor
Mehvash Fatima

Technical Editor
Ankita Thakur

Copy Editor
Sonia Cheema

Project Coordinator
Milton Dsouza

Proofreader
Safis Editing

Indexer
Hemangini Bari

Graphics
Jason Monteiro

Production Coordinator
Nilesh Mohite

Cover Work
Nilesh Mohite

About the Author

Krzysztof Rakowski has 13 years of professional experience in IT as a team leader, software developer and architect, and agile project manager. During the course of his career, he has helped major global brands establish their online presence using scalable, fault-tolerant, and high-performance systems. His broad experience comes from various industries, including interactive advertising, banking, retail, and e-commerce. He is a recognized expert, Zend Certified Engineer, and a Professional Scrum Master.

Currently, Krzysztof works for the largest online shop in central and eastern Europe — where he is responsible for supervising teams of software engineers and project managers who pair the smartest IT solutions with the best customer experience.

He enjoys sharing his knowledge through articles and presentations. He occasionally writes about his side projects on his website at `www.rakowski.pro`.

In his free time, Krzysztof likes to travel around the world with his wife, go snowboarding, or read a good book.

I would like to thank my wife, Anna, for her constant support, encouragement, and patience. I also want to thank my parents, parents-in-law, and brother for inspiring me to reach my goals.

This book wouldn't be possible without the generous support of the friendly people at Packt Publishing.

About the Reviewer

Faisal Rahman is a developer, writer, mentor, and tech enthusiast. His passion extends from architecting secure, scalable, and maintainable software to finding optimal algorithms and data structures for the smallest problems in a system. His research on optimization algorithms for known mathematical problems has been published in reputed journals. He is currently working as a software engineer at Microsoft.

www.PacktPub.com

Support files, eBooks, discount offers, and more

For support files and downloads related to your book, please visit www.PacktPub.com.

Did you know that Packt offers eBook versions of every book published, with PDF and ePub files available? You can upgrade to the eBook version at www.PacktPub.com and as a print book customer, you are entitled to a discount on the eBook copy. Get in touch with us at service@packtpub.com for more details.

At www.PacktPub.com, you can also read a collection of free technical articles, sign up for a range of free newsletters and receive exclusive discounts and offers on Packt books and eBooks.

https://www2.packtpub.com/books/subscription/packtlib

Do you need instant solutions to your IT questions? PacktLib is Packt's online digital book library. Here, you can search, access, and read Packt's entire library of books.

Why subscribe?

- Fully searchable across every book published by Packt
- Copy and paste, print, and bookmark content
- On demand and accessible via a web browser

Free access for Packt account holders

If you have an account with Packt at www.PacktPub.com, you can use this to access PacktLib today and view 9 entirely free books. Simply use your login credentials for immediate access.

I dedicate my work on this book to my son, Ignacy, who will be born as this book goes into print.

Table of Contents

Preface

In 2007, Facebook's engineers needed to integrate the various applications powering their website. As their engineering culture encouraged selecting the best tools for a task without imposing strict rules regarding the choice of technology, their applications were written in a wide spectrum of different programming languages, which were considered the best for the given task.

Looking for the best solution to fulfill their needs, the engineers reviewed lots of different frameworks that were already available on the market. None of them was deemed sufficient in terms of performance or flexibility. They made a decision to develop their own solution, which became a standard to integrate all the services on Facebook.

As they considered their solution to be exceeding the current standards of the market, they released their code to the open source community, passing the task of maintaining their work on the project to the Apache Software Foundation. Since then, Apache Thrift has been developed by a large group of volunteers.

Now you can use Apache Thrift as a tool to expose your own services that are written in different languages and make your applications communicate with each other. Regardless of whether you intend to work on a small-scale application or huge enterprise, Apache Thrift may be one of the best tools for you.

In *Learning Apache Thrift*, you will find an introduction to various concepts of the services around you and some service-oriented architecture (SOA). Then you will learn how to use Apache Thrift in various projects. We will discuss advanced concepts too to see how the giants of the industry use this framework, and you will get some solid advice and much needed inspiration.

What this book covers

Chapter 1, Introducing Apache Thrift, gives you basic information about the environment where services are needed. You will learn about the history of Apache Thrift and its position in the market. This chapter provides some solid understanding of the context in which Apache Thrift exists.

Chapter 2, Installing and Running Apache Thrift, provides you with a quick tutorial that will allow you to have Apache Thrift up and running on your machine in no time. Instructions for Linux (Debian and CentOS), Windows, and Mac OS X are included.

Chapter 3, Running Your First Apache Thrift Service and Client, gives you the ability to see Apache Thrift in action. Simple instructions will get you through the process of setting up a server and client that run in two different programming languages (PHP and Python) and communicate with each other.

Chapter 4, Understanding How Apache Thrift Works, provides you with real knowledge of the framework's internals. You will learn about its components, network stacks, data types, interface description language (IDL), and the programming languages that are supported. You will also find out about its limitations and how to deal with them. This chapter is essential to understand the concept of "under the hood", and how to design your own Apache Thrift-supported services.

Chapter 5, Generating and Running Code in Different Languages, provides you with a toolbox of essential information about different popular programming languages and how you can use them with Apache Thrift. You may read it from the beginning to the end or just focus on those languages that interest you. The same example is used for every language, so you can easily compare the server's and client's implementation for each of them.

Chapter 6, Handling Errors in Apache Thrift, gives you information on how to deal with undesirable situations that may occur when you run your service or client. Handling errors is an important part of any programming project, and is especially essential when dealing with cross-platform applications where errors occur frequently due to the nature of the distributed architecture.

Chapter 7, An Example Client-Server Application, gathers knowledge from the whole book into one example client-server application. You will build the code step by step. The example touches every aspect of Apache Thrift and is a bit more complicated than what you have done until now. Three different languages will be used (PHP, Python, and Ruby).

Chapter 8, Advanced Usage of Apache Thrift, inspires you to further expand your Apache Thrift skills. You will learn how big companies use this framework, how to run your applications in production, and how to address security, performance, and scalability issues. You will be also be given access to other interesting Apache Thrift-related projects.

What you need for this book

To run the examples in this book, you will need any modern computer running Linux—CentOS or Debian (preferred)—Mac OS X, or Windows. You will also need some text editor to edit your code.

You will also need an Internet connection to download Apache Thrift and other required software on your computer.

Who this book is for

If you have some experience of developing applications in one or more languages that are supported by Apache Thrift (C++, Java, PHP, Python, Ruby, and others) and want to broaden your knowledge and skills in building cross-platform, scalable applications, then this book is for you.

Conventions

In this book, you will find a number of text styles that distinguish between different kinds of information. Here are some examples of these styles and an explanation of their meaning.

Code words in text, database table names, folder names, filenames, file extensions, pathnames, dummy URLs, user input, and Twitter handles are shown as follows: "It initializes the variable x, which is an integer."

A block of code is set as follows:

```
int main()
{
    int x = 42;
    // this line will produce compilation error
    x = "forty two";
    return 0;
}
```

Any command-line input or output is written as follows:

```
sudo apt-get update
```

New terms and **important words** are shown in bold. Words that you see on the screen, for example, in menus or dialog boxes, appear in the text like this: "It varies from version to version, but in most cases may be found if you right-click on **My Computer** and choose **Properties**, then look for the **Advanced** panel and the **Environment Variables...** tab."

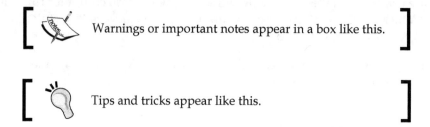

Warnings or important notes appear in a box like this.

Tips and tricks appear like this.

Reader feedback

Feedback from our readers is always welcome. Let us know what you think about this book—what you liked or disliked. Reader feedback is important for us as it helps us develop titles that you will really get the most out of.

To send us general feedback, simply e-mail feedback@packtpub.com, and mention the book's title in the subject of your message.

If there is a topic that you have expertise in and you are interested in either writing or contributing to a book, see our author guide at www.packtpub.com/authors.

Customer support

Now that you are the proud owner of a Packt book, we have a number of things to help you to get the most from your purchase.

Downloading the example code

You can download the example code files from your account at http://www.packtpub.com for all the Packt Publishing books you have purchased. If you purchased this book elsewhere, you can visit http://www.packtpub.com/support and register to have the files e-mailed directly to you.

Errata

Although we have taken every care to ensure the accuracy of our content, mistakes do happen. If you find a mistake in one of our books—maybe a mistake in the text or the code—we would be grateful if you could report this to us. By doing so, you can save other readers from frustration and help us improve subsequent versions of this book. If you find any errata, please report them by visiting http://www.packtpub.com/submit-errata, selecting your book, clicking on the **Errata Submission Form** link, and entering the details of your errata. Once your errata are verified, your submission will be accepted and the errata will be uploaded to our website or added to any list of existing errata under the Errata section of that title.

To view the previously submitted errata, go to https://www.packtpub.com/books/content/support and enter the name of the book in the search field. The required information will appear under the **Errata** section.

Piracy

Piracy of copyrighted material on the Internet is an ongoing problem across all media. At Packt, we take the protection of our copyright and licenses very seriously. If you come across any illegal copies of our works in any form on the Internet, please provide us with the location address or website name immediately so that we can pursue a remedy.

Please contact us at copyright@packtpub.com with a link to the suspected pirated material.

We appreciate your help in protecting our authors and our ability to bring you valuable content.

Questions

If you have a problem with any aspect of this book, you can contact us at questions@packtpub.com, and we will do our best to address the problem.

1
Introducing Apache Thrift

There is a milestone in the life of every sufficiently large application that marks the point when it is too big to be maintained as a monolith. For some systems, it is in their blueprints from the very beginning, while for others, it comes as a growth induced necessity and brings along the need for massive rebuild.

Apache Thrift is one of the tools that assist in building scalable, distributed systems, spanning across different platforms and languages. Originally developed for internal use by Facebook, now it is an open source software project backed by the Apache Foundation. It is characterized by a wide range of supported languages, flexibility, and performance.

In this chapter, you will learn about the scenarios where using Apache Thrift may be necessary. You will also get familiar with its basic properties and how it is compared to other similar frameworks. It is essential to know the big picture to be able to select the best tool for your job.

Let's see how you can put Apache Thrift to good use!

Distributed systems and their services

Imagine typical web applications that you use every day, such as search engines, messaging platforms, or social networks. Under one web address, they deliver different services. For example, a social network delivers people search, messaging, and users' profile pages. While you access them by one user interface—a web page written in HTML and JavaScript—what you see in your browser is only a gateway. Your request to message a friend is being relayed by the underlying application to the messaging service—an application which is specifically designed to deal with exchange of messages between the social network's users.

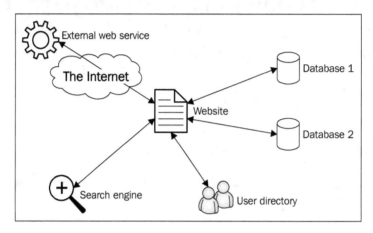

Service-oriented architecture

Messaging service, which we use as an example here, may be written in a completely different programming language than web application. It is a design decision. The system architect may decide that interface of your social network; the web pages that you see every time you log in will be easier to manage and maintain when they are written in, let's say, PHP or Ruby on Rails. However, messaging systems may be written in Python as the architect may decide that this language offers better libraries for this task. On the other hand, search engines or other tools that need superb performance are often written in C++. There may be also some internal corporate applications in Java or C#.

Those applications, of course, need to communicate with each other. But how to do that? There is a concept in software design called **service-oriented architecture** (**SOA**). We just discussed the first part of this principle. It focuses on creating applications around distinct tasks. If every task is performed by a different application, there is a need for some means of communication between them. To achieve this goal, applications expose services that are used by other applications. Typically, they are accessible over some medium, that is, an internal network or the Internet. They are self-contained and autonomous, which means they are independent of other services and are able to deliver complete response when queried. They should also be well documented so that any developer can use them.

Distributed systems

When — as in our example of social network — we have a system that consists of many autonomous services, we call such systems **distributed systems**. Depending on the scale, business needs, or technical constraints, the systems may be spread over lots of computers in a local network, the Internet, or just on a single machine. Benefitting from the SOA principles, you may run and test on your desktop computer distributed system of the same logical architecture, which will be then used on hundreds of servers in the production environment.

There are many advantages of SOA in distributed systems over monolithic applications. Let's discuss some of them.

Maintainability

The greatest advantage of distributed systems in SOA is their maintainability, which means ease of performing all the tasks related to the caretaking of the software. If the system consists of many applications, each dedicated to one task or type of tasks instead of one big monolith, some of the actions can be performed a lot easier:

- You can select tools (that is, programming languages, libraries, and services) that are best for a given task. You can use different toolsets for search engine, message queues, or data-intensive calculations.

- Instead of having all the developers working on one application (that means one code base), you can split the team to work on many applications separately. You can even outsource some of the work to external teams or companies. This way, they won't get in each other's way. Smaller teams are more agile and yield better results.

- Communication between the different components of the system is narrowed to only one specified interface, which is easier to comprehend, monitor, and debug than lots of convoluted classes and methods.

- It is easier to respond to failures and fix bugs. Let's say there's some bug introduced that causes whole application to crash. In distributed systems, only one service may be down, while the whole system is operational. System operators or developers are able to replace the service with the stable version and do some tests to identify the bug or perform other actions without affecting the rest of the system.

- Introducing changes is a lot easier too. In the common workflow, if a new version of a service is to be deployed, it can be run as a separate instance with the old version simultaneously. System operators can switch the client application from the old to the new service and see whether everything performs correctly. If it does, the old service is turned off; otherwise, it is easy to switch back to the old service and fix the new one. It is even easier in the cloud environments.

Scalability

Many systems are required to perform well under a high load. It is not only the domain of web applications, but it is best pictured here: popular websites receive hundreds of millions of page views per day, which constitutes a high traffic load. To withstand such increasing stress, systems need to scale. The most obvious way, known by every computer user, is to add RAM or switch to a better CPU if applications don't run smoothly. But there is a limit to such scaling (called **vertical scaling**). You don't expect Google to run on a single powerful computer, do you?

The other type of scalability is **horizontal scaling**, which means adding more computers (called **nodes**) to the system. For example, our imaginary social network system may consist of several web application nodes, a few database nodes, and also some user search nodes. In properly designed systems, operators can add or remove nodes depending on the expected load and other circumstances. More sophisticated systems can even scale themselves, starting or stopping nodes in the cloud automatically, based on the traffic analysis.

SOA allows multiple nodes of the same function to be accessible to the clients. As services are self-contained, independent of the state of other services, and documented, developers can prepare their software without much care if they will be dealing with one or hundred nodes. In most scenarios, traffic to the services is managed by software or hardware load balancers, making it completely invisible for the client.

Testability

Another advantage of distributed systems is the easiness of testing them and finding and fixing bugs. Independence of services means that they can be tested in isolation from the whole system. Only a particular service's operation is being tested without any influence from other components. Because services should be well documented, it is easy to predict the desired output for a given input. If bugs are found, they can be evaluated and fixed without the need to consider them in the scope of whole system.

An introduction to Apache Thrift

You probably know Facebook, the popular social network. A small website started in 2004 as a funny side project by a Harvard student, Mark Zuckerberg, gained huge popularity, having more and more users. In its early years it faced rapid growth in terms of traffic, system, and network structure. Their engineering culture allowed choosing any solution that was deemed optimal for a given task without any constraints or standards. This led to a situation when they had lots of different services, but no reliable way to connect them together. Describing Apache Thrift, Facebook's engineers stated in the white paper (you can download it from `https://thrift.apache.org/static/files/thrift-20070401.pdf`):

> *"(...) we were presented with the challenge of building a transparent, high-performance bridge across many programming languages."*

They tested solutions available in the market and came to the conclusion that none of them fulfilled the requirements of high performance, flexibility, and simplicity. The result of their work was Thrift—a piece of software that was later open sourced and handed over to the Apache Foundation.

Apache Thrift's simplicity comes from the fact that the code for different programming languages is generated automatically from a single file written in the **interface definition language** (IDL). In other similar solutions, data has to be prepared before it is transferred to meet the limitations of the method of transport—not all structures are easily transferred. In most cases, simple data types such as strings are integers and transferrable. Due to this, a developer has to translate every structure more complex than that to the text form in a process called **serialization**. This has to be done on both ends (deserialization being the reverse process), which needs extra work, testing, and debugging. In the case of Apache Thrift, the developer can use data types native to their programming language of choice using the methods dedicated to this language. All serialization and deserialization is made by the Apache Thrift itself and is not visible to the developer. This architecture of the solution allows programmers to focus on working on the actual services, and not having to care about how the data is going to be transferred from one application to another.

Let's have a quick glance at the pillars of Apache Thrift. Some of the topics will be covered in much more detail in *Chapter 4, Understanding How Apache Thrift Works*, so here are just the basics that you will need to understand our first code examples.

Supported programming languages

Before starting any work with Apache Thrift, you should probably check whether it supports the programming language that you use. Of course, there is a great chance that it does—most of the popular languages are supported. The complete list for version 0.9.3 is as follows:

- ActionScript 3
- C++
- C#
- D
- Delphi
- Erlang
- Haskell
- Java
- JavaScript
- Node.js
- Objective-C/Cocoa
- OCaml
- Perl
- PHP
- Python
- Ruby
- Smalltalk

> Note that Apache Thrift is still in the pre-1.0 version, so some of the languages may be not fully supported. It is best to check on the Apache Thrift website (https://thrift. apache.org/docs/features), in the source code, or try to learn the current status of support for your favorite programming language yourself.

If your language of choice is on the list (especially if it is a popular one), you can be sure that you will be able to generate all the code necessary to work with Apache Thrift.

Data types

One of the basic features of every programming language is their data types. Although the basic ones may be very similar, that is, integer or string, it may not be that easy for the rest of them. Some of the languages (for example, C++) are statically typed. This means that the type of the variable has to be known at the compile time. Thus, it has to be defined in the source code when the program is written. After that, the variable can be of only this type. For example, consider the following line from C++:

```
int x = 42;
```

It initializes the variable x, which is an integer. This variable has to stay an integer through the execution of the program. If later on you would like to assign a value of some other type, it will produce an error as soon as you compile your program. Let's take a look at the following example:

```
int main()
{
    int x = 42;
    // this line will produce compilation error
    x = "forty two";
    return 0;
}
```

If you try to compile this simple code, you will end up with the following compile error:

```
$ g++ -o example example.cpp
example.cpp: In function 'int main()':
example.cpp:4:6: error: invalid conversion from 'const char*' to 'int'
[-fpermissive]
     x = "forty two";
       ^
```

Other languages are dynamically typed, that is, the type of the variable is checked in the runtime, but in the source code it might be anything, any time. Consider this example from PHP:

```
if (rand(0,1) == 1) {
    $x = 42;
} else {
```

```
        $x = "forty two";
    }
    var_dump($x); // var_dump() function prints type of specified
                  // variable and its value
```

Depending on the random outcome of the condition, the value of the variable may be either integer or string. Let's take a look at the following example:

$ php -f example.php

The result of running this program would be either `string(9)` `"forty-two"` or `int(42)`.

As you can see, both values are permitted as PHP interpreter changes the type of the variable during the runtime.

Programming language allows that and, moreover, later on, you can assign values of different types to the same variable.

Without Apache Thrift, developer would have to serialize the variables. It means that before the variables are transferred, they should be mapped to the most basic data types that are understood by every programming language (most probably, integers and strings of characters). After the transmission, those serialized variables have to be translated back to the structures available in the programming language at the receiving end.

Apache Thrift does all that dirty work for the developer. It provides its own data types that are then mapped to the ones native to the given programming language, thereby allowing the developer to focus on creating the application, not the communication interface.

Transports

Transports are a part of Apache Thrift's network stack. They allow you to transmit data over different channels, that is, HTTP protocol, sockets, or files. Decoupling the transport layer lets you to easily choose the transport that best fits your solution without many changes in the code.

The choice of transport should be dictated by the architecture of your solution.

Protocols

Protocols prepare data to be transmitted over transports. The name of the process is called **serialization** (when sending data) and **deserialization** (when receiving data). There are different protocols that can be used: JSON, binary, plain text, and so on. It means that depending on what data you want to transfer, you can use different methods of serialization. For example, if you expect to transmit images or other binary data, choosing the binary protocol is the best option as there would be almost zero overhead. If you chose JSON for this purpose, binary data would be converted to text, thereby increasing the payload by a third or more.

The choice of protocol should be dictated by the data you wish to transfer using Apache Thrift.

Versioning

Versioning is an approach for managing changes in the service's API (and in the software in general). As software is being developed, it changes. Sometimes the changes are miniscule, and sometimes great. They are often manifested by modification of the methods or parameters exposed by the API.

When developing client and server software, you shouldn't assume that clients will be updated to the newest version instantly. It is not possible, even if you have total control of the environment. It is also wise to allow the older versions of the client to work with the newer versions of the server.

Changes in the APIs, libraries, and other externally available components pose a big challenge for the developers, leading to problems often referred to as **dependency hell** — when different applications are compatible with different versions of the same library or API, leading to difficulties with managing those dependencies.

To alleviate this inconvenience, most of the software developers adopt a convention of marking the version of the application with decimal numbers, according to the template, MAJOR.MINOR.PATCH, where PATCH means miniscule changes (that is, fixing some bugs), MINOR is a larger change but backward-compatible with the previous versions, and MAJOR means a major release that might break the compatibility with the previous versions of the software.

Apache Thrift's feature is soft versioning. It means that there are no formal requirements as to how the changes between the subsequent versions should be handled or announced. However, it delivers a set of tools that allows users to easily keep backward compatibility with the new versions of the service. It is achieved by the following properties:

- The method's arguments are numbered. You can add or remove them. As long as the same number is not reused, the new versions of methods may function without removed arguments. Those numbers shouldn't be changed for any existing argument.

- You can set default values for the arguments, so if the older version of the client has a method without a new variable, the service doesn't receive any value for such an argument and the default value is set. This is useful when you want to add some fields.

- While manipulation with fields is relatively easy, you shouldn't rename methods or services. This makes them unavailable for the older clients.

Security

Security is essential to every service. Although you definitely need to take extra care when exposing services to the Internet, it is also important when they are available in private networks.

Apache Thrift allows you to use `TSSLTransportFactory` to utilize RSA key pairs, providing security for the connection.

Another way of securing your Apache Thrift connection (although a little bit more complicated) is tunneling it over SSH.

We will discuss this in the detail in *Chapter 8, Advanced Usage of Apache Thrift*.

Interface description language

Apache Thrift's core feature is its own IDL, one that shapes its simplicity and usability. It will be familiar at first sight to anyone who has programmed in contemporary programming languages. Using IDL, you are able to define the service and all the variables that it uses in one file. It is an unambiguous description of what the service will look similar to without going into the implementation details.

Let's consider a very simple service, which allows you to add two integers:

```
namespace py thrift.example1
namespace php thrift.example1
```

```
service AddService {
    i32 add(1: i32 a, 2: i32 b),
}
```

This example code defines `AddService` service, which contains the `add` method. This method takes two 32-bit signed integers (i32) as parameters and also returns such an integer as a result. We will want to have the code generated for Python and PHP languages, but of course Apache Thrift is able to do it for a far greater spectrum of languages.

Now the Thrift's magic begins; if you save this code to the file (let's say, `example1.thrift`) and run the following commands, you will get the code of client and server for this service in desired languages (Python and PHP in this example) in the newly-created folders, `gen-py` and `gen-php`:

```
$ thrift --gen py example1.thrift
$ thrift --gen php example1.thrift
```

In the simplest solution, it is enough to fill the code of the `add` method, and voilà, you have a fully-functional client and server.

This example is, of course, oversimplified, but shows the major advantage of Apache Thrift—the ability to define in one place and then instantly generate services and the corresponding client code without the need of writing code in every language from scratch. It is a great tool not only for final solutions, but also for rapid prototyping for different programming languages.

To see how much work Apache Thrift just spared you, examine the generated files that are saved in the `gen-py` and `gen-php` folders.

IDL is a very powerful tool. It has a lot of options and gives you a great deal of flexibility. We will discuss it in greater detail in *Chapter 4*, *Understanding How Apache Thrift Works*.

Apache Thrift and others

Until now, you may have come to the conclusion that Apache Thrift is the best solution for all your needs when dealing with distributed systems. Surprisingly, it is not always true. In this section, we will review similar tools so that you are able to understand how Apache Thrift compares to them and when to use which tool.

Custom protocols

Frequently, inventing your own custom protocol is the first idea that comes to a developer's mind when he/she needs to transfer data between two applications. Very often, it works surprisingly well in small solutions, which are not expected to scale or be modified frequently.

Examples of such solutions are popular in web applications. Creating your own custom protocol is as simple as generating output with some text: just plain or formatted according to JSON or XML specification, and serving it through HTTP. On the client side, we need to connect to this service, get the content, and parse it.

To imagine such a solution better, consider a very simple example of a service adding two numbers. The request may be the following GET call:

```
GET /add?number1=30&number2=12
```

The response in the JSON format may be the following:

```
{"result":42}
```

Unfortunately, the only advantage of such solutions is that they are quick and easy to implement, both on the server- and client-side, on a small scale. Besides that, there are some disadvantages:

- Text-based protocols have significant overhead. This is especially true for XML, which encapsulates everything with lots of tags.

- They transfer binary data (that is, images), adding additional overhead to the payload. As those protocols are text-based, binary data has to be converted to text. One of the popular techniques is Base64, which encodes the message byte by byte into a printable text character. The outcome of such an operation is that the string that is ready to be transferred is around 37% larger than the original binary data. There is also extra processing required on both client's and server's end.

- There are really no standards for such protocols; everything has to be invented by the developer. It poses not only difficulty when designing such a service, but also is a complication when the client's applications have to be maintained; for every service, there need to be custom tools prepared. And no standards means that debugging is a lot more difficult.

- Maintenance is another problem with such protocols. When there is a change needed, both server and client code needs to be modified separately and deployed at the same time. There is no way to modify the code once and have it working on both client and server.

Of course, the spectrum of possibilities when designing custom protocols is much wider than those examples that are typical for web applications. One can design their own binary protocols working on sockets, files, queues, or another medium. This gets rid of some of the disadvantages of text-based protocols, but still leaves lots of other problems to deal with.

XML-RPC and JSON-RPC

XML-RPC is one of the early **remote procedure call** (**RPC**) protocols, which uses XML-encoded messages transferred over HTTP. JSON-RPC is its much younger cousin, which is based on the same principle, but uses JSON instead of XML.

Both protocols allow you to call remote services with handful of data types in the relevant format. The exchanged messages are plain XML or JSON without any overhead.

Here is an example of a typical XML-RPC request:

```
<?xml version="1.0"?>
<methodCall>
    <methodName>add</methodName>
    <params>
        <param>
            <value>
                <int>30</int>
            </value>
        </param>
        <param>
            <value>
                <int>12</int>
            </value>
        </param>
    </params>
</methodCall>
```

And, the corresponding response is:

```
<?xml version="1.0">
<methodResponse>
    <params>
        <param>
            <value>
                <int>42</int>
            </value>
        </param>
    </params>
</methodResponse>
```

JSON-RPC request is much more verbose:

```
{"method": "add", "params": [30, 12], "id": 1}
```

The service will return the following response:

```
{"result": 42, "error": null, "id": 1}
```

The simplicity of both of these protocols comes at a price. While they may be easily implemented, they share disadvantages of custom protocols, such as lack of standards and need for maintenance of both server and client codes, and they may not be best suited for transferring binary data.

SOAP and WSDL

Simple Object Access Protocol (SOAP) is a solution for some problems with customarily designed protocols, which evolved from XML-RPC. It is used mainly for web services (over HTTP) to exchange structured information between them and clients.

SOAP is a protocol based on XML. It is rather complicated with several layers of specification. The messages are structured according to this specification.

Every SOAP message consists of the following elements:

- **Envelope**: This is the root element of the message that identifies the message as SOAP and defines its structure.
- **Header**: This is an optional field that may contain extra application-specific control information for identifying the message.
- **Body**: This contains the actual payload of the message (call or response).
- **Fault**: This is an optional element that is used to pass information about errors. It contains error code, description, and other application-specific information.

Web services over the Internet are commonly provided with SOAP as a method of calling operations described in the **Web Services Description Language (WSDL)** file. In this file, the available messages are described in the XML schema form.

Due to SOAP's standardization it is easy to debug, and there are many tools that help to do that. It is enough to parse the WSDL file to be able to communicate with the given web service.

Unfortunately, SOAP still has disadvantages discussed previously: a large overhead connected to XML processing and the need to encode binary data into text form.

RESTful APIs

WSDL-based web services using SOAP were considered cumbersome and complex, so **Representational State Transfer** (**REST**) was introduced as a simpler alternative. Web services that are developed in accordance with REST's architecture constraints are called **RESTful APIs**.

Features of REST can be perceived as a mix of two previously discussed topics: custom protocols and SOAP.

RESTful APIs are simpler and a lot lighter than SOAP. They make use of HTTP methods to manipulate the data (collections of elements):

- GET: This is used to retrieve information about some collection or its elements
- PUT: This is used to create or replace the collection or element
- POST: This is used to create a new element in the collection
- DELETE: This is used to delete entire collection or a specific element

Every collection or its element has its own, unique **Universal Resource Identifier** (**URI**).

The advantages of RESTful APIs are their simplicity and efficiency. They are also scalable and cacheable.

On the side of disadvantages, there is a lack of standardization (each service's message and response format may be different), no built-in error handling, and no standardized authentication mechanisms.

CORBA

Common Object Request Broker Architecture (**CORBA**), http://www.corba. org/, dates back to 1991, and is the oldest of the standards presented in this chapter. However, its concepts are quite similar to Apache Thrift (for example, it uses its own IDL).

It is considered a bit cumbersome; instead of using a language's native code, a developer needs to use a CORBA-specific one. It's hard to install and heavy to run. There are different implementations and they are inconsistent.

Apache Avro

Apache Avro (https://avro.apache.org/) is another remote procedure call and data serialization framework developed with the support of the Apache Foundation. It was developed as a tool for the Apache Hadoop framework.

Lots of similarities to Apache Thrift include describing the interface with IDL, support for many programming languages (Java, C, C++, C#, Scala, Python, and Ruby), and a compact, fast binary format.

The main difference is that Avro's code doesn't have to be generated when the service is defined and later on, when it changes. It could be, for statically typed languages, but for dynamically typed languages, it is not necessary. It is possible because Avro uses the dynamic schema, which accompanies data when it is being transferred.

As a disadvantage in comparison with Apache Thrift, Apache Avro doesn't offer such a wide selection of serialization formats (protocols, in Thrift's terminology) and transports.

Protocol Buffers

Protocol Buffers are an *older brother* of Apache Thrift, and they share lots of similarities. They were developed as an internal proprietary software in Google and are used in most of the inter-machine communication. Since their release to open source in 2008, they have gained support not only for officially implemented languages (C++, Java, and Python), but also a lot more (JavaScript, Go, PHP, Ruby, Perl, and Scala).

Apart from IDL syntax and implementation details, Protocol Buffers differ from Apache Thrift in that they have less language support, different base types, a lack of constants and containers, and no built-in exception handling. In the open source version, there is also no RPC implementation for services (you need to implement it yourself).

On the other hand, Protocol Buffers are a little bit faster than Apache Thrift and their objects are smaller. Also the documentation and availability of tutorial is considered better and more complete.

When to choose Apache Thrift

When designing and developing applications that have to communicate with each other, one may go through the whole evolution process involving the solutions presented in the previous section. Many services start as a very limited tool, which works quite well with some simple custom protocol. But the data that needs to be transferred may become more and more complicated than the need for some format, such as JSON or XML appears JSON-RPC or XML-RPC may be then used.

As the service is growing and is exposed to more external applications, the need to standardize the architecture and proper documentation arises. In such cases, using web services based on SOAP and WSDL seems to be a proper idea. If your application's goal is to operate on collections of elements, RESTful API may be a good solution.

But there are situations where one needs to transfer binary data and provide flexibility for changing the definition of the services along with support for different platforms and languages; all this in an environment where high performance is crucial. In these cases, serialization and remote procedure call for frameworks such as Apache Avro, Protocol Buffers, and Apache Thrift. From these three, the last one offers the widest selection of serialization formats, and transports along with remote procedure call implementation.

Summary

Distributed systems, SOA, SOAP, WSDL, XML, and JSON, are some of the popular buzzwords that are frequently encountered by developers interested in creating applications that talk to each other. It is often hard to comprehend how these theoretical concepts can be used to accomplish the goal.

In this chapter, we learned what these distributed systems are and Apache Thrift's role in achieving communication between different services. We also discussed its position among similar solutions and their advantages and disadvantages.

In the upcoming chapters, we will install Apache Thrift, generate and run our simple services, and discuss the features in great detail. Having this knowledge, we will advance to prepare our own client-server application using Apache Thrift.

2

Installing and Running Apache Thrift

In this chapter, we will go through the installation process for Apache Thrift on the three most popular platforms: Linux, Mac OS X, and Microsoft Windows. All the required software and libraries are free and downloadable from the Internet, so just to follow the instructions for your platform is enough.

After completing this chapter, you will have a working environment and compile your first file written in the Apache Thrift's IDL.

Apache Thrift's official documentation is specific about the versions of the software it requires. Although you should be successful with different versions (especially newer), in case of any trouble, your best bet is to try out the versions specified here.

> The development and release process for any software is often more rapid than the process of writing and publishing the book. This version of the installation guide is based on and tested with Apache Thrift's 0.9.2 version. If you run into any trouble, you should refer to the current requirements specification on the Apache Thrift's official website at
> https://thrift.apache.org/docs/install/.

Installing Apache Thrift on Linux

Apache Thrift is officially supported on Debian and its flavors (including Ubuntu) and CentOS. Of course, it is also possible to install it on different distributions as the instructions are pretty straightforward and can be easily ported—the main requirement is a POSIX-compliant system.

Note that you need to have root privileges on your machine as some libraries and software probably need to be updated. The commands requiring such privileges are prefixed with sudo.

For the sake of the brevity of this manual, the output of the given commands is omitted in most cases where it is not relevant. You should be OK as long as the command results in success.

Installation requirements

On the Linux platform, you will need to build your Apache Thrift compiler from the source. It requires the following tools (version numbers are minimal versions recommended by Apache Thrift's developers):

- g++ 4.2
- boost 1.53.0
- autoconf 2.65
- automake 1.13
- libtool 1.5.24
- pkg-configautoconf macros (pkg.4)
- lex and yacc runtime libraries
- libssl-dev

There are also a few extra minimal requirements for programming languages:

- C++
    - libevent (to build a non-blocking server)
    - zlib

- Java 1.7
    - Apache Ant

- C#: Mono 1.2.4
- Python 2.6 or newer (including header files for extension modules)
- PHP 5.0 or newer (optionally including header files for extension modules)
- Ruby 1.8 or newer
    - bundler gem

- Erlang R12 (it also works on R11, but it's not recommended by Apache Thrift's creators)
- Perl 5

- ○ Bit::Vector
- ○ Class::Accessor

- Haxe 3.1.3 or newer
- Go 1.4 or newer
- Delphi 2010

It is possible to disable some of the programming languages during the compilation process. You will learn how to do it in the upcoming sections.

Installing dependencies

Before actually compiling Apache Thrift, you need to install all the required dependencies. Since Linux distributions use different package managers and different versions of software, instructions vary.

Most of the required packages are provided through package management systems of the distributions; only in some cases, you need to compile them manually.

The following instructions are as extensive as possible, including all the requirements that are needed to install Apache Thrift and some of the problematic scenarios you may face. It was tested on fresh installations of CentOS 7 and Ubuntu 14.04 LTS. However, due to Linux's nature—a multitude of distributions, versions, and the uniqueness of each machine—some problematic situations (for example, compile errors) may occur. In such cases, you will need to resolve them yourself. Fortunately, more often than not, someone has already had the same problem, so your help may be one Google search away.

If you want just to play with Apache Thrift and see how it works, I recommend working not on your regular machine, but on a virtual one created just for this purpose. A virtual machine is—as the name states—a virtual computer (called **guest**) with many capabilities such as network connection or the ability to read CD discs, and it runs on your own physical computer (called **host**). The advantage is that you don't change any software on your current machine. You can always create a snapshot (a kind of "save game") and in case of misfortune start from there or just scrap the whole virtual machine and start from scratch.

A great tool to run virtual machines is the open source Oracle VirtualBox (`http://www.virtualbox.org/`) and proprietary (but free for personal use) VMware Player Pro (`http://www.vmware.com/products/player/`). To run a new Linux instance, you need to install one of them, create a new virtual machine, and provide Linux ISO image, which you can download from `http://www.ubuntu.com/download/desktop`. This process is really straightforward and can easily be completed by following the in-application instructions.

Installing dependencies on CentOS

This instruction is valid for CentOS 7, but should be also applicable to any newer version and a few older. Follow these steps:

1. First of all, make sure that your system is up to date. If needed, the newest versions of software can be installed. To do this, use the following command:

   ```
   $ sudo yum -y update
   ```

2. Then, install the Development Tools. It's a group of essential development tools that are needed if you want to compile your own applications:

   ```
   $ sudo yum -y groupinstall "Development Tools"
   ```

   Some of the languages need extra libraries if you want to write and run clients and servers in them. These requirements were listed previously, so here, we'll just list the commands needed to install them. If you already have some of this software in your computer, it will be skipped. Some of the actions require wget (a tool needed to download files from the Internet).

3. If you don't have wget installed, do it now with the following command:

   ```
   $ sudo yum -y install wget
   ```

4. Now, let's install the required dependencies for C++:

   ```
   $ sudo yum -y install libevent-devel zlib-devel openssl-devel
   boost-devel bzip2-devel
   ```

5. You also need to upgrade boost to the version newer than the one supplied by yum. To do this, run the following commands:

   ```
   $ wget http://sourceforge.net/projects/boost/files/boost/1.58.0/
   boost_1_58_0.tar.gz
   $ tar -xvzf boost_1_58_0.tar.gz
   $ cd boost_1_58_0
   $ sudo ./bootstrap.sh
   $ sudo ./b2 install
   ```

6. For Java, you will need Java Development Kit (in this instance, OpenJDK) and Apache Ant. Install it using the following command:

   ```
   $ sudo yum -y install java-1.7.0-openjdk ant
   ```

7. For PHP, the interpreter is needed:

   ```
   $ sudo yum -y install php
   ```

8. Similarly, for Python use this:

   ```
   $ sudo yum -y install python
   ```

9. For Ruby, you will need interpreter, development libraries, and some development tools, such as `gem`, `rake`, `bundler`, `rspec`, and `rdoc`:

```
$ sudo yum install ruby rubygems ruby-devel rake
$ sudo gem install bundler rspec rdoc
```

10. If you need to work with Node.js, you will need the newest version, which is not provided by the package manager. You need to download the source code, and compile and install it yourself:

```
$ wget https://nodejs.org/dist/v0.12.7/node-v0.12.7.tar.gz
$ tar -xvzf node-v0.12.7.tar.gz
$ cd node-v0.12.7
$ ./configure
$ make
$ sudo make install
```

After completing these steps, you will have everything that is needed to compile and install Apache Thrift.

Installing dependencies on Debian and Ubuntu

This instruction is valid for Ubuntu 14.04 LTS and Debian 8.1 Jessie. Ubuntu and Debian share a package manager (Ubuntu being based on Debian), so the instructions are similar. Moreover, they should work for Ubuntu's variants (such as Kubuntu, Xubuntu, Lubuntu, and so on.)

First of all, make sure that your system is up-to-date. To do this, update the package list and upgrade your system:

```
$ sudo apt-get update
$ sudo apt-get upgrade
```

Then, install or update the necessary libraries:

```
$ sudo apt-get install libboost1.54-all-dev libevent-dev g++ bison
libssl-dev
```

As with CentOS, some of the languages need extra libraries if you want to write and run clients and servers in them. These requirements were listed previously, so here, we'll just list the commands needed to install them. If you already have some of this software in your computer, it will be skipped. Some of the actions require `wget`. If you don't have `wget` installed, do it now:

```
$ sudo apt-get install wget
```

Python should be enabled by default. If not, install it with the following command:

```
$ sudo apt-get install python
```

For PHP, you will need only the command-line interpreter:

```
$ sudo apt-get install php5-cli
```

If you want to be able to run PHP scripts as a web application, you may want to install the php5 package (which also installs the apache2 package—Apache HTTP Server):

```
$ sudo apt-get install php5
```

To install Node.js, you can use:

```
$ sudo apt-get install nodejs npm
```

For Java, you have a few options. If you haven't installed Java previously, you should run the javac command to see the list of the possible Java packages. The result will look similar to this:

```
The program 'javac' can be found in the following packages:
 * default-jdk
 * ecj
 * gcj-4.8-jdk
 * openjdk-7-jdk
 * gcj-4.6-jdk
 * openjdk-6-jdk
Try: sudo apt-get install <selected package>
```

You may choose any JDK you want; we will use OpenJDK for our tutorials. We will install it together with Apache Ant, which is also on the list of the requirements:

```
$ sudo apt-get install openjdk-7-jdk ant
```

For Ruby, you will need interpreter, development libraries, and some development tools, such as gem, rake, bundler, rspec and rdoc:

```
$ sudo apt-get install ruby rake ruby-dev gems
$ sudo gem install bundler
```

After completing these steps, you will have everything that is needed to compile and install Apache Thrift.

Installing Apache Thrift

At this stage, you should have anything that is needed to compile and install Apache Thrift on your CentOS, Ubuntu, or Debian Linux machine.

1. First, let's download the newest version of the software. Go to the download page at `https://thrift.apache.org/download` and click on the link at the top of the page (at the time of writing, it was **thrift-0.9.2.tar.gz**) for the latest stable release of Apache Thrift. This link will take you to the page that serves you the source page that is geographically closest to you. Copy the link and supply it to `wget`:

    ```
    $ wget http://www.eu.apache.org/dist/thrift/0.9.2/thrift-
    0.9.2.tar.gz
    ```

2. After the download completes, decompress the archive and switch the directory:

    ```
    $ tar -xvzf thrift-0.9.2.tar.gz
    $ cd thrift-0.9.2
    ```

    Now you will work in this directory to configure, compile, and install Apache Thrift. If any problems occur after troubleshooting, most likely you will have to repeat the process from this point.

3. Let's run the configure script:

    -   `./configure`: This script checks your environment and looks for the required dependencies. There will be a lot of information printed on the screen. If something is missing, you will get the error message.

4. To help you debug the configuration process, you may want to familiarize yourself with the modifiers available for the configuration script:

    -   `./configure --help`: There are lots of them, but in the beginning, you will need only a few. For example, if some of your dependencies are installed in non-standard locations or configure can't find them (you will know by the error messages), you may need to specify their exact location in either `--with-zlib=/usr/include` or `--with-boost=/usr/local` way.

Sometimes, you may want to skip some languages. To do that, you can use `--without-<language>` option, for example:

```
$ ./configure --without-php
```

One of the popular instances is a problem with the Lua programming language, which occurs during compilation:

```
libtool: link: gcc -shared  -fPIC -DPIC  src/.libs/libluasocket_la-
luasocket.o src/.libs/libluasocket_la-usocket.o   -llua5.2 -lm -lssl
-lcrypto -lrt -lpthread  -O2   -Wl,-soname -Wl,libluasocket.so.0 -o
.libs/libluasocket.so.0.0.0
/usr/bin/ld: cannot find -llua5.2
collect2: error: ld returned 1 exit status
```

As it is highly unlikely that your first Apache Thrift application will be in Lua, you may want to skip it by using the following option:

```
$ ./configure --without-lua
```

If you want to stick with Lua, you need to update it from source as current repositories for Ubuntu, Debian, and CentOS don't provide the required 5.2+ version.

You may also encounter a problem with the `configure` script properly recognizing your `boost` library. In such situations, check where it is on your machine:

```
$ whereis boost
boost: /usr/include/boost
```

Then supply this information to the configure script:

```
$ ./configure -with-boost=/usr/include/boost
```

Of course, you may use more than one argument at a time.

The most important output of the configure script is at the end. It lists all the programming languages that it was able to configure. The information looks similar to this:

```
thrift 0.9.2

Building C++ Library ......... : yes
Building C (GLib) Library .... : no
Building Java Library ........ : yes
Building C# Library .......... : no
Building Python Library ...... : yes
Building Ruby Library ........ : yes
Building Haskell Library ..... : no
Building Perl Library ........ : no
Building PHP Library ......... : yes
```

```
Building Erlang Library ...... : no
Building Go Library .......... : no
Building D Library ........... : no
Building NodeJS Library ...... : yes
Building Lua Library ......... : yes


C++ Library:
    Build TZlibTransport ...... : yes
    Build TNonblockingServer .. : yes
    Build TQTcpServer (Qt) .... : no


Java Library:
    Using javac ............... : javac
    Using java ................ : java
    Using ant ................. : /usr/bin/ant


Python Library:
    Using Python .............. : /usr/bin/python


PHP Library:
    Using php-config .......... :


Ruby Library:
    Using Ruby ................ : /usr/bin/ruby


NodeJS Library:
    Using NodeJS .............. : /usr/local/bin/node
    Using NodeJS version....... : v0.12.7


Lua Library:
    Using Lua ............. : /usr/bin/lua
```

If something is missing that you think should be present, skim the output of configure to find the missing component; the details are present in `config.log`.

As you may see in the preceding output, all the supported languages, some additional information about used executables, and so on are listed. This is the point where you should check whether the programming language of your choice is enabled on the list. If not, check whether you followed all the instructions in the *Installing dependencies* section. You may also want to check the `config.log` file, which stores the detailed information about the progress of the configure script. Look for the keywords connected with your language, for example, `ruby` or `cpp`.

When you are satisfied with the output of the configure script, now is the time for the compilation. It may take few minutes (depending on your machine), so grab a coffee and run this command:

```
$ make
```

It may ask for your password to compile and install system-wide dependencies (that is, for Ruby).

Sometimes, the compiler may complain about missing files with an error message similar to this:

```
Makefile:1048: gen-cpp/.deps/ChildService.Plo: No such file or directory
Makefile:1049: gen-cpp/.deps/DebugProtoTest_types.Plo: No such file or
directory
Makefile:1050: gen-cpp/.deps/EnumTest_types.Plo: No such file or
directory
Makefile:1051: gen-cpp/.deps/OptionalRequiredTest_types.Plo: No such file
or directory
Makefile:1052: gen-cpp/.deps/ParentService.Plo: No such file or directory
Makefile:1053: gen-cpp/.deps/Recursive_types.Plo: No such file or
directory
Makefile:1054: gen-cpp/.deps/ThriftTest_constants.Plo: No such file or
directory
Makefile:1055: gen-cpp/.deps/ThriftTest_types.Plo: No such file or
directory
Makefile:1056: gen-cpp/.deps/TypedefTest_types.Plo: No such file or
directory
Makefile:1057: gen-cpp/.deps/proc_types.Plo: No such file or directory
make[1]: *** No rule to make target 'gen-cpp/.deps/proc_types.Plo'.
Stop.
make: *** [check-recursive] Error 1
```

To resolve this issue, it may be helpful to disable the parallel make and set the `-j` parameter to 1, which means that the compiler will run in a single job only:

```
$ make -j 1
```

When the compilation is complete, it's time for the last step—the installation of the compiled files in your system. To do this, issue the following command:

```
$ sudo make install
```

We noticed that to avoid certain privilege errors on CentOS, you may need to use:

```
$ su -
$ make install
```

Also, when you select Ruby as one of the languages, this method will yield errors similar to this (even if you have rdoc installed):

```
Successfully installed thrift-0.9.2.0
ERROR:  While executing gem ... (Gem::DocumentError)
    RDoc is not installed: cannot load such file -- rdoc/rdoc
rake aborted!
Command failed with status (1): [gem install thrift-0.9.2.0.gem...]
```

To suppress the error and go on with the installation process, you need to use the -i argument:

```
$ make -i install
```

When this process succeeds, you have Apache Thrift installed on your system. To check, just run the following command:

```
$ thrift
Usage: thrift [options] file
Use thrift -help for a list of options
```

If your output is similar to the preceding, congratulations; you have installed Apache Thrift on your Linux box!

Installing Apache Thrift on Mac OS X

Mac OS X, being a Unix-based system, offers a very similar experience to Linux systems. However, it doesn't contain an out-of-the-box, Apple-supported package management system such as yum or apt-get. Fortunately, there is a great third-party, open source replacement called **Homebrew** (http://brew.sh/). It is a great tool, especially for users familiar with Linux package managers. I recommend it not only to manage Apache Thrift, but also other packages that you may need.

To install Homebrew, just use the clever script provided on their website:

```
$ ruby -e "$(curl -fsSL https://raw.githubusercontent.com/Homebrew/
install/master/install)"
```

Alternatively, if you don't like running arbitrary code downloaded from the Internet, you can follow the step-by-step instructions at the following link, which will give you some alternatives for how to perform the installation:

```
https://github.com/Homebrew/homebrew/blob/master/share/doc/homebrew/
Installation.md
```

When you have Homebrew installed, you can use it to install dependencies:

```
$ brew install boost openssl
```

Installing Apache Thrift

Now you can install Apache Thrift. First, check the package to see the available bindings you would like to install as well:

```
$ brew info thrift
```

This will yield a result similar to:

```
thrift: stable 0.9.2 (bottled), HEAD
http://thrift.apache.org
/usr/local/Cellar/thrift/0.9.2 (90 files, 5.4M) *
  Poured from bottle
From: https://github.com/Homebrew/homebrew/blob/master/Library/Formula/
thrift.rb
==> Dependencies
Build: bison ✗
Required: boost ✔, openssl ✔
==> Options
--with-erlang
  Install Erlang binding
--with-haskell
  Install Haskell binding
--with-java
  Install Java binding
--with-perl
  Install Perl binding
--with-php
  Install PHP binding
```

```
--with-python
  Build with python support
--HEAD
  install HEAD version
==> Caveats
To install Ruby binding:
  gem install thrift
To install PHP extension for e.g. PHP 5.5:
  brew install homebrew/php/php55-thrift
```

As you can see, you may choose some bindings. Use them when installing Apache Thrift:

```
$ brew install thrift --with-python --with-php
```

If you want to have Ruby binding, do it by installing the relevant `gem` (you may need to use `sudo`):

```
$ gem install thrift
```

Check your Apache Thrift installation by running the following command:

```
$ thrift
Usage: thrift [options] file


Use thrift -help for a list of options
```

If your output looks similar, you're good to go!

Installing Apache Thrift on Windows

Although primarily designed for Unix-compatible systems, Apache Thrift can also be used in the Windows environment. The installation is very easy; it is enough to download the Thrift compiler from the download page, `https://thrift.apache.org/download`. No installation is needed; you may work directly with the downloaded file. For consistency, I suggest renaming the file that you downloaded (that is, `thrift-0.9.2.exe`) to just `thrift.exe`. In order to be able to run this command from any directory on your computer, add this file's location to the PATH environment variable. (It varies from version to version, but in most cases, it may be found if you right-click on **My Computer** and choose **Properties**. Then, look for the **Advanced** panel and the **Environment Variables...** tab. If in doubt, the solution can be found easily on Google).

If you want to develop applications that use Apache Thrift, you, most likely, will be using Visual Studio and C++ or C# bindings. They are provided in the subdirectories of lib in your Apache Thrift archive with the relevant Visual Studio project files.

Testing the installation

To test whether Apache Thrift is installed and works properly, we will generate some code for a service, which does nothing. Don't worry we will get straight to your first fully-working application in Chapter 3, *Running Your First Apache Thrift Service and Client*. Now is the time to just check whether everything is in place.

Use the following code in Apache Thrift's IDL and put it in some file, that is, test.thrift:

```
# this is just a Test service, which contains two methods

service Test {

    # this method probably does nothing
    void donothing(),

    # this method probably multiplies two numbers
    i32 multiply(1:i32 number1, 2:i32 number2),

}
```

Downloading the example code

You can download the example code files for all Packt books you have purchased from your account at http://www.packtpub.com. If you purchased this book elsewhere, you can visit http://www.packtpub.com/support and register to have the files e-mailed directly to you.

As you may see, we defined a simple service called Test. It contains two methods: one called donothing, which doesn't return anything (void), and the other, multiply, which takes two arguments of type i32 (which is 32-bit signed integer)—number1 and number2—and also returns a 32-bit signed integer.

At this stage, it doesn't matter what the methods do; they even don't have to be implemented (you will learn more detail in Chapter 4, *Understanding How Apache Thrift Works*). To see if you did everything properly, run the following command in the directory where you saved your `test.thrift` file:

```
$ thrift --gen php --gen py test.thrift
```

The command that you just ran takes the `test.thrift` file, parses it through the Apache Thrift compiler, and generates service files in PHP and Python languages that you may use to develop your services.

The default output directory is `gen-<language_name>`; so in this case, the directories are `gen-php` and `gen-py`. Check whether these directories were created, and in fact, whether there are some PHP or Python files. If yes, congratulations; your Apache Thrift was installed successfully!

As an extra task, I encourage you to browse through the files and see the vast amount of work that Apache Thrift does for you while you don't need to write a single line of code yet.

Summary

In this chapter, we learned how to compile and install Apache Thrift on various environments such as Linux, Mac OS, and Windows. We also learned about other software and dependencies that the installations require, and how to check a successful installation by running commands. Now you have everything you need to start creating your first application.

In the next chapter, you will run your first Apache Thrift client and service with examples and instructions.

3
Running Your First Apache Thrift Service and Client

As you have everything ready, we shouldn't wait any longer to let you run your first Apache Thrift-enabled application.

The plan for this chapter is that firstly, you will create the necessary project files. After a brief configuration, you will be able to run the service and connect it with the client by yourself. We will be using a server written in PHP and a client in Python. The code is very simple, so you can adapt it to any other programming language if you wish.

At the end of this chapter, we will discuss the code and exactly what it means. Don't worry if you don't understand everything at the beginning. The goal of this chapter is to allow you to have a running client and service that you can easily manipulate and change. We will discuss the technical details in *Chapter 4, Understanding How Apache Thrift Works*.

Creating necessary project files

Let's make a fresh start by creating a new directory on your disk. In this directory, we will keep all the files related to the current chapter's mini project.

Creating a local copy of the Apache Thrift libraries

To make things simpler, we will make a local copy of the Apache Thrift libraries.

Copy the archive that you downloaded in the previous chapter to your newly-created directory and decompress it:

```
$ tar -xvzf thrift-0.9.2.tar.gz
```

Note for Windows users

In the examples, we will use Unix-style commands as this is the most popular platform for Apache Thrift. Use Windows equivalents when needed.

To decompress the `.tar.gz` archives under Windows, I recommend suitable open source (free) software, for example, 7-Zip, which you can download from `http://www.7-zip.org/`.

Now we will have full Apache Thrift in the `thrift-0.9.2` directory (the name may differ depending on the version; substitute it in all the commands). We will be using PHP and Python libraries that are in the `thrift-0.9.2/lib` directory.

The Python library needs to be built. Enter its directory and run the `setup` command. This library will not be installed system-wise; just build in place:

```
$ cd thrift-0.9.2/lib/py
$ python setup.py build
$ cd ../../..
```

Defining our first service and generating files

Now we're back in our main directory and ready for the real work. Here is the description of the service, `MyFirstService`, that we will be working on. Note that Apache Thrift's IDL only describes the interface without really providing any information about what the methods will be doing. It is the service developer's responsibility to make sure that the names of the services and methods are consistent with what they are actually doing.

You don't have to type all the code by yourself. You can download it from Packt's website and use it in your project.

Let's look at the interface description:

```
// namespaces are used in resulting packages
namespace php myfirst
namespace py myfirst
```

```
// you can define names for your types.
// Usable primarily for integers.
typedef i32 int

// simple exception
exception MyError {
    1: int error_code,
    2: string error_description
}

// here starts the service definition
service MyFirstService {

    // log method - it saves timestamp to given file
    oneway void log(1:string filename),

    // multiply method - returns result of multiplication of two
integers; it returns integer as well
    int multiply(1:int number1, 2:int number2),

    // get_log_size method -  returns size of log file; throws
exception when problems occur
    int get_log_size(1:string filename) throws (1:MyError error),

}
```

As you can see, in MyFirstService, we described three methods:

- oneway void log(1:string filename): This will save some value
  (timestamp in our example) to the given file
- int multiply(1:int number1, 2:int number2): This will multiply two
  integers and return the result
- int get_log_size(1:string filename) throws (1:MyError error):
  This will return the size of given log file and in case of any trouble, it will
  throw an exception

We will get to the details later. Now save this code in the myfirst.thrift file. As
a next step, use Apache Thrift compiler that you installed in the previous chapter to
generate PHP and Python files:

```
thrift --gen py --gen php:server myfirst.thrift
```

This command will generate lots of PHP files in the gen-php directory and Python files in the gen-py directory. You can browse them and admire how much work Apache Thrift does for you. Of main interest for us are the gen-php/MyFirstService.php and gen-py/MyFirstService.py files, which contain (among others) definition of the interface that we have to implement by ourselves in PHP and client classes.

The service code in PHP

At this point, we have everything that Apache Thrift can offer automatically. The next step is to prepare the code for our service. In a real-world scenario, this probably will be a part of larger application. Now, as a demonstration, we will have an extremely basic setup and its main purpose is to be portable and easy to run.

> Note that in order to be simple and comprehensive, code in this chapter may lack features that need to be taken care of in professional applications, which are meant to be used in real-world solutions. For example, there is not much validation or input sanitization, errors are not always properly handled, and the application may not perform well under heavy load.
>
> If you plan to use this or similar code in your applications, please apply general knowledge related to application security and performance characteristics to your programming language.
>
> In *Chapter 8, Advanced Usage of Apache Thrift*, you will learn some essential information about running Apache Thrift applications in production.

Let's have a look at our server's code:

```php
#!/usr/bin/env php
<?php

error_reporting(E_ERROR);
date_default_timezone_set('UTC');

define('THRIFT_PHP_LIB', __DIR__.'/thrift-0.9.2/lib/php/lib');
define('GEN_PHP_DIR', __DIR__.'/gen-php');

require_once THRIFT_PHP_LIB.'/Thrift/ClassLoader/ThriftClassLoader.php';

use Thrift\ClassLoader\ThriftClassLoader;
```

```php
$loader = new ThriftClassLoader();
$loader->registerNamespace('Thrift', THRIFT_PHP_LIB);
$loader->registerDefinition('myfirst', GEN_PHP_DIR);
$loader->register();



use Thrift\Protocol\TBinaryProtocol;
use Thrift\Transport\TPhpStream;
use Thrift\Transport\TBufferedTransport;

class MyFirstHandler implements \myfirst\MyFirstServiceIf {

    public function log($filename) {
        $time = date('Y-m-d H:m:s');
        file_put_contents(__DIR__."/".$filename, $time."\n", FILE_
APPEND);
        error_log("Written " . $time . " to " . $filename);
    }

    public function multiply($number1, $number2) {
        error_log("multiply " . $number1 . " by " . $number2);
        return $number1 * $number2;
    }


    public function get_log_size($filename) {
        $filesize = filesize(__DIR__."/".$filename);
        if ($filesize === false)
            {
                $e = new \myfirst\MyError();
                $e->error_code = 1;
                $e->error_description = "Can't get size information
for file " . $filename;
                error_log($e->error_description);
                throw $e;
            }
        error_log("size of log file " . $filename . " is " . $filesize
. "B");
        return $filesize;
    }

};
```

```
header('Content-Type', 'application/x-thrift');
echo "\r\n";


$handler = new MyFirstHandler();
$processor = new \myfirst\MyFirstServiceProcessor($handler);

$transport = new TBufferedTransport(new TPhpStream(TPhpStream::MODE_R
| TPhpStream::MODE_W));
$protocol = new TBinaryProtocol($transport, true, true);

$transport->open();
$processor->process($protocol, $protocol);
$transport->close();
```

Don't get scared by the broadness of this file. We will discuss it in detail later. Basic knowledge of any programming language will let you easily see that here we are implementing three methods (log, multiply, and get_log_size) that were just briefly described in the IDL file. There is some PHP code that performs the basic operations promised by the methods' names.

Save this code to the MyFirstServer.php file. Make sure that the path to the Apache Thrift library in the line 7 is correct:

```
define('THRIFT_PHP_LIB', __DIR__.'/thrift-0.9.2/lib/php/lib');
```

If you want the timestamps in the log file to reflect your time zone (helpful for debugging), set a proper identifier in line 5:

```
date_default_timezone_set('UTC');
```

 You may check the list of available time zone identifiers at http://php.net/manual/en/timezones.php.

You may run this code via a regular web server (that is, an Apache HTTP server or nginx) if you have it set up. If not, there is a simpler solution in a few lines of Python that is suggested in Apache Thrift's code library:

```
#!/usr/bin/env python

import os
import BaseHTTPServer
import CGIHTTPServer

class Handler(CGIHTTPServer.CGIHTTPRequestHandler):
```

```
    cgi_directories = ['/']

print "Starting server on port 8080..."

BaseHTTPServer.HTTPServer(('', 8080), Handler).serve_forever()
```

This code uses Python's native capabilities to serve files from the local directory via HTTP on port 8080. They will be parsed as a CGI script, that is, the PHP code will be interpreted by the PHP interpreter, and that's exactly what we need. Save this code to the runserver.py file.

> Note that you shouldn't use this method for running the PHP scripts in a production environment. It's not reliable and doesn't provide adequate performance. Also, it may be vulnerable in terms of security. It's intended only as a helper to developers.
>
> Instead, you should run your PHP scripts in one of the ways recommended and extensively explained in the PHP documentation at http://php.net/manual/en/install.php.

The client code in Python

As we have the service code, now it's time to have some code for the client. This small Python script will connect to the service exposed by PHP and run some methods from MyFirstService. Let's see how simple that is:

```
#!/usr/bin/env python

import sys, glob
sys.path.append('gen-py')
sys.path.insert(0, glob.glob('thrift-0.9.2/lib/py/build/lib.*')[0])

from myfirst import MyFirstService

from thrift import Thrift
from thrift.transport import THttpClient
from thrift.transport import TTransport
from thrift.protocol import TBinaryProtocol

from random import randint

try:

    socket = THttpClient.THttpClient('localhost', 8080, '/
MyFirstServer.php')
```

```
transport = TTransport.TBufferedTransport(socket)
protocol = TBinaryProtocol.TBinaryProtocol(transport)
client = MyFirstService.Client(protocol)
transport.open()

# calling log method
client.log("logfile.log")
print 'logged current time to logfile (not waiting for response)'

# calling multiply method with random parameters
number1 = randint(1,100)
number2 = randint(1,100)
product = client.multiply(number1,number2)
print '%dx%d=%d' % (number1, number2, product)

# calling get_log_size method
    print "current size of logfile is: %d Bytes" % client.get_log_
size("logfile.log")

# calling get_log_size method second time, but this time with
wrong parameter
    print "current size of logfile is: %d Bytes" % client.get_log_
size("no_such_file.log")


    transport.close()

except Thrift.TException, e:
    print 'Received following error:\n  error code: %d\n  error desc:
%s' % (e.error_code, e.error_description)
```

After a brief analysis of the code, you may see that we are using an instance of the `MyFirstService.Client` class that implements the same methods that we had defined in our PHP service. Running remote code is as easy as calling methods of this instance.

Note that we send random values to the `multiply` method to illustrate that every request is different. Also, in the second calling of the `get_log_size` method, we provide the name of the file that doesn't exist, so we have an opportunity to see how errors are handled.

Save this code to the `client.py` file.

Running the code

Now is the time to run the scripts and see the outcome. It is best to use two separate terminal windows so that you can observe the result of the operation on both client and server side.

To start your PHP service, you need to run it through the Python wrapper that you wrote. To do this, run the following command:

```
$ python runserver.py
Starting server on port 8080...
```

If you see a message like this and no other error, it means that your PHP service is listening on the port 8080 on your computer. In this window, you will see information about all the incoming connections and their results.

Now, let's try to call our service with Python client script. To do this, run the following command:

```
$ python client.py
```

If everything happened as expected, you will see some output. It will look similar to this:

```
logged current time to logfile (not waiting for response)
70x7=490
current size of logfile is: 760 Bytes
Received following error:
   error code: 1
   error desc: Can't get size information for file no_such_file.log
```

In the first terminal (the one, where you ran your server), you will see messages similar to this:

```
127.0.0.1 - - [04/Aug/2015 23:05:59] "POST /MyFirstServer.php HTTP/1.0"
200 -
Written 2015-08-04 23:05:59 to logfile.log
127.0.0.1 - - [04/Aug/2015 23:05:59] "POST /MyFirstServer.php HTTP/1.0"
200 -
multiply 22 by 52
127.0.0.1 - - [04/Aug/2015 23:05:59] "POST /MyFirstServer.php HTTP/1.0"
200 -
size of log file logfile.log is 20B
```

```
127.0.0.1 - - [04/Aug/2015 23:05:59] "POST /MyFirstServer.php HTTP/1.0"
200 -
```

```
Can't get size information for file no_such_file.log
```

It is a regular access log with extra information delivered by the PHP script.

You can run the client script multiple times, just to see the different results. You will also notice that `logfile.log` was created on the disk in the same directory where the script is located, and is appended with the current time every time you run the client script.

What really happened?

Let's talk a little about what really happened here.

At the beginning, you ran the `runserver.py` script. It doesn't play a huge role here; it is just a little helper Python script. Its purpose is to run continuously and listen on the `8080` port of your computer and serve files from the current directory over HTTP without all the hassle of setting up a regular web server. It runs them as the CGI scripts, so our PHP file is going to be parsed by the PHP interpreter installed on your system.

When we have the server running, we can connect to it. To do this, you ran the `client.py` script. This piece of code benefits from the capabilities of Apache Thrift. Using autogenerated libraries, it allows you to call remote commands from your Python script. In this case, you asked to run the following methods:

- `log("logfile.log")`
- `multiply(number1, number2)`, where both numbers were randomly chosen from the range of 1 to 100
- `get_log_size("logfile.log")`
- `get_log_size("no_such_file.log")`

Those requests were sent to the `http://localhost:8080/MyFirstServer.php` address and they were passed by our helper script to the `MyFirstServer.php` script. There, they were executed. The running `log` method resulted in appending the current time to `logfile.log` (you can see it by yourself); `multiply` yielded the result of the multiplication of the two numbers that you provided; and `get_log_size` returned the size of the log file at the first call and at the second (where the non-existent filename was given), it threw an exception, which was transferred from the PHP server to the Python client and handled there.

In general, what you have seen here is that the procedures were called remotely. They were implemented in the PHP script, but were invoked from, and the result was processed in an independent Python script. In this simple example, everything occurred on one machine, but it could work equally well between computers spread all over the world.

The purpose of Apache Thrift in this example is to provide a communication framework and automatically generate libraries so that the developer doesn't have to worry about serializing and transfer methods (and lots of other stuff) and he/she can focus on implementing the service and client.

Analyzing the code

Before we go further, let's have a quick look and explain the most important parts of the code that we used in this chapter. We will dig deeper into the technical details and deal with many useful Apache Thrift options in *Chapter 4*, *Understanding How Apache Thrift Works*.

The service description – IDL

The most important part of the service description begins with the following line:

```
service MyFirstService {
```

In this block, there are descriptions of methods exposed by this service. Let's have a look at the first two:

```
oneway void log(1:string filename),
int multiply(1:int number1, 2:int number2),
```

The syntax bears a strong resemblance to C++'s (and other popular languages') method definitions. The `oneway` keyword means that the client only makes a request and won't wait for the result of the `log` method. This method doesn't provide any return value, which is marked by the `void` keyword (note that all `oneway` methods should return `void`). You may also notice numbered argument notation that is typical for Apache Thrift.

The `multiply` method, on the other hand, returns `int`, which is the name defined by us for the not intuitively named type of `i32`, which is a 32-bit signed integer.

The `get_log_size` method also returns `int`, but has one distinct feature:

```
int get_log_size(1:string filename) throws (1:MyError error),
```

It throws `MyError`, which means that in case of a failure, it will throw an exception that we defined earlier in the file.

The server script – PHP

Our service is implemented in PHP. Lots of Apache Thrift-specific code surrounds the most important part, which is the implementation of our service's interface:

```
class MyFirstHandler implements \myfirst\MyFirstServiceIf {
```

The `MyFirstHandler` class has the same methods as the ones described in our IDL file. It is essential that the names of the methods and parameters (and their order) are the same; otherwise, you won't be able to call them.

Implementations of the methods are very simplistic and lack lots of essential features (such as error handling or input validation), but serve their purpose of providing some output to the client. An extra output is also sent through the `error_log` function to the terminal window in which you run `runserver.py`.

The code preceding and following the `MyFirstHandler` class prepares the environment for running the script and defines how the data will be transferred. We will discuss it in great detail in *Chapter 5, Generating and Running Code in Different Languages.*

The client script – Python

You may have noticed that in the client script, the transfer details are the same as in the server script. It's the same transport (`TBufferedTransport`) and protocol (`TBinaryProtocol`). The script will connect to the port, `8080`, on local host.

The most important part of this script is the client object. It has the same methods as those provided by the server, so you can just run them without giving a second thought to how the data is transferred between the client and the server. The return values are native to Python, and exceptions are handled just the same way as in any other application in this language.

Activity for you

As an extra task, I encourage you to play with the service and the client. Try to change the code of methods in the PHP file. Issue different calls from the client Python file. Add extra methods to your service and handle them in the client (remember to do it in the service definition in the `myfirst.thrift` file as well and generate the needed libraries using the `thrift` command). You may even want to add some extra error handling or throw an exception or two.

Summary

In this chapter, you implemented your first service in the PHP language and a client script in Python. You ran the client, called the service's methods remotely, and examined the output. I hope that you experimented a little bit with your scripts.

After reading this chapter, you are now able to prepare the development environment, implement services, and make use of them through the client application.

In the next chapters, we will get into the technical details, which will allow you to fully understand Apache Thrift's potential and make use of it!

4
Understanding How Apache Thrift Works

Now that you ran your first service and client with Apache Thrift, it's time to learn about how it really works and what options you can choose when designing your application. In this chapter, we will go through the Apache Thrift's building blocks.

First, we will cover Apache Thrift's architecture, how does it look from the developer's perspective, as well as its internal structure.

Next, you will learn about Apache Thrift's variable types, the building blocks of every interface description. From basic types, such as integers and strings, through more complex types, such as struct, to the service, which are combinations of all of them.

In conclusion, we will go through the last piece of the puzzle — the definition of IDL syntax. Knowing all this will allow you to construct your own IDL files.

Prepare your tools

To benefit from this chapter, you should be able to run the Thrift compiler frequently, be able to review the generated files and test your changes. We will be working on the `myfirst.thrift` file, which was prepared in the previous chapter. I encourage you to test different data types, service definitions, compile them, and examine the generated code.

> Note that on Windows computers, your Apache Thrift compiler will be named `thrift.exe`.

Apache Thrift's architecture

Apache Thrift's architecture can be viewed from two angles. The first approach shows the tool that is used by the developer—the Thrift compiler—along with the set of instructions that determine what to do in order to run the services.

The second way is to get to know the internal architecture and the purpose of protocols, transports, services, and processors that the developer will use, in order to know how the tools are built and what are the ways of their operation.

As in every craft, you can build things knowing the basic operation of the tool that you will work with; not every developer needs to have a deep knowledge of Apache Thrift's internals to do his job. However, to fully understand how it works and design the scalable and performant services and system architectures, this knowledge is essential.

If you wish to get the information about Apache Thrift IDL syntax and start preparing your services right away without getting too much into the technical details, you may want to skim over this section or skip it altogether and go straight to the section about the type system.

However, I highly recommend every developer to get back to this section some time later to learn essential information that definitely will be needed in the future.

Going about using the tool

One of Apache Thrift's advantages is that it is rather simple to use and implement in the programs written in many different programming languages. Developers are able to apply a simple instruction set in order to have the services and clients up and running in no time.

Let's have a look at the schema illustrating the typical workflow:

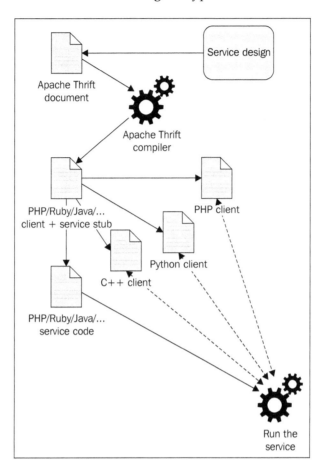

In this section, we will discuss the following steps:

- Designing the services
- Preparing interface description
- Generating the service and client libraries
- Implementing services and clients
- Running the server and clients

Note that this section describes the developer's workflow with Apache Thrift and its purpose is to draw a general picture of the process. Detailed information about specific commands, parameters, and so on, can be found in other chapters in the book.

Designing the services

First, the most important step is independent of the software; it is to design your system and services. In a typical scenario, you would need to assess the applications that are already in place or be developed. It has to be taken into consideration that what kind of interaction between them is needed. Most commonly the applications would need to do one of the two things, that is, either receive or deliver some data or perform some operations remotely.

It is possible that there will be one or many such services exposed in your system.

Frequently in the typical production setup, some applications may be accessible to other applications, others not. Sometimes, the communication may be permitted only in one direction. This is often due to security restrictions, company policy, or network topology. Take this into consideration when designing services and making the decision about which application should expose them and which should act as a client.

Preparing the interface description

After you reviewed your needs and designed your services, you need to prepare the Apache Thrift document, which is written in IDL and has the .thrift extension. You will describe each of the services. To do this, first you need to define variables and constants that you will use. Service description offers the information about the functions, their parameters, the kind of value they return, and if they can throw an exception. In one file, there can be multiple services described.

You learned about how the exemplary Apache Thrift document looks like in the previous chapter. More on the syntax of this document is in the upcoming sections.

Generating service and client libraries

When your interface description document is ready, you can run the `thrift` command with the required parameters on your IDL document. This command takes the file, processes it and generates — in accordance with different specifications for each of the programming languages — the files containing description of the services and related variables' types that will be used by your service and clients. These files extend the classes delivered by the Apache Thrift library.

If you will go through the generated files, you will see that every element from your IDL document was translated to the programming language of your choice. We will examine these files in detail in *Chapter 5, Generating and Running Code in Different Languages*.

Implementing services and clients

This step is sometimes perceived as the hardest part, as the developer is required to prepare the server's and client's code from scratch, and the documentation is sometimes sparse on this subject.

The first step is to implement the services and wrap them around in the server's code. This code will be based heavily on the Apache Thrift library and the generated classes. You need to choose the desired processor, transport, and protocol (more on this in later sections) and add the actual functions' code. In real life, this code will rely hugely on the different parts of your application. However, for the sake of brevity, the client and server code is self-contained (with the exception of any language's standard libraries) throughout this book.

The second step is to implement the clients. As with the server, you are required to do it by yourself from scratch. This time, however, it is easier: you need to pick the same type of processor, transport, and protocol as you choose for the server and instantiate the service class generated by the compiler.

In most cases, you will implement the services only in one programming language as a part of the application delivering those services. The client's code, on the other hand, may be implemented in many languages depending on the different applications that need to access your service.

You have seen the example code of the server and client in the previous chapter.

Running server and clients

You run your server's and clients' code in a way typical for the programming language of your choice. Remember to start the server first and then run the clients.

As you may see, Apache Thrift removes the burden of preparing the communication from scratch; you just need to fill in the gaps that are prepared for you to have a fully functional, cross-language communication.

The network stack

You now know how the Apache Thrift works from the outside. Let's look at the internals that let your applications to communicate. The purpose of the network stack is to allow getting your message through various communication layers and encapsulating the message along the way. The variables are serialized to the form that can be eventually sent through the network or other medium. The form of serialization is decoupled from the transport layer. After the message is transmitted, it is received by the client and then deserialized.

An easy way to understand the network stack is to imagine a traditional postal system. When you want to send a letter to your friend on the other side of the world, you don't expect that someone will pick up the single sheet of paper from you, carry it around and then after some time, hand it to your friend. You need to prepare your letter to its journey through various layers of the postal system or, as we may say in this context, encapsulate it.

First, you put it in the envelope, which specifies the delivery address, and insert it into the mailbox. When the mailman comes, he opens the mailbox and puts the letters in the bag in the back of his truck. Then, at the various levels/layers of the postal system, your letter is sorted, put in the different bags or containers, and shipped by trucks or trains to the central sorting centers. When it's the time to hop over the ocean, the bag with your letter will be probably put in some bigger container and safely placed in the airplane's cargo bay.

When the plane arrives to the country of the destination, the process is reversed: the bags are unloaded from the cargo container, delivered through the different sorting centers to the destination post office, where the postman takes his bag and puts your letter in your friend's delivery box. The last step is performed by the recipient, who tears the envelope and reads the letter — the same piece of paper that you wrote.

Apache Thrift's network stack consists of transport, protocol, processor, and server.

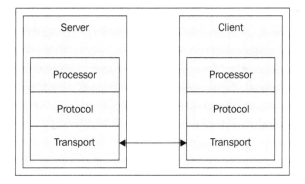

Let's look at those components.

Transport

The transport layer provides a way to read and write data from and to the network or any other medium that you want to use. It is independent from the protocol, so you are able to separately choose how you will serialize the data to be transferred.

Apache Thrift offers a wide spectrum of transports that could be used depending on the architecture of your solution. Their availability is not consistent; some are widely available while others only in selected languages. The documentation is also sparse, sometimes even none; one has to look through the implementation source code to work out the details.

To make your life easier at this point, here is a collection of basic transports that are most common and allow you to successfully communicate between your applications.

All of the transports implement Apache Thrift's `TTransport` interface in respective programming languages. Some of the transports are end point transports (it means they write and read directly to or from the device) others are layered transports (it means they are chained with other transports).

The following transports are widely supported:

- `TSocket`: This uses a blocking socket, which means that only one connection can be active at a time. Thus, it is not a very good solution for production.

- `TPhpStream` (only in PHP): This is useful in situations when we have HTTP server running (that is, Apache or nginx) and want to output the result of the PHP script through this server without actually running our own server.

- `TBufferedTransport`: Other transports are often wrapped around in this one, as it provides buffering of input and output data.

- `TFramedTransport`: This is also a wrap-around layer to provide framing of the payload.

- `TFileTransport` (or `TFileObjectTransport` in Python): This is used to read and write to the file.

You will learn more about the availability of specific transports in various programming languages in *Chapter 5, Generating and Running Code in Different Languages*, and in *Chapter 8, Advanced Usage of Apache Thrift*, we will discuss how to make your connection secure by wrapping it around in the TLS/SSL encryption.

 When choosing the transport for your application, it is important to make sure that it is implemented in the programming languages that you would like to use. If you plan to establish the communication between the applications in the same language and you are sure that it will stay this way, you may go with the specialized transports available for you. But if you plan to make it cross-language, your best bet is those more popular.

Protocol

Protocol is responsible for mapping the in-memory structures (simple and complex data types) to a format that can be transmitted over the selected transport. This process is called serialization (or **encoding**) when transmitting the message and deserialization (or **decoding**) when receiving it. Protocol is independent of the transport used.

Protocols in Apache Thrift face the same issues as the transports; there is a wide offer that can be matched to your architecture. However, protocols' availability is inconsistent and very often there is lack of documentation; the developer needs to look through the source code to figure out the details.

This is a list of the most popular protocols:

- `TBinaryProtocol`: This is a simple protocol that converts all data to binary values. You should use it if you don't have any specific needs, as this one is the most universal.
- `TCompactProtocol`: This Apache Thrift's own protocol uses a lot of optimizations to make the payload as small as possible.
- `TJSONProtocol`: The payload is encoded as a JSON string.

All of the transports implement Apache Thrift's `TProtocol` interface in respective programming languages.

You will read learn more about the availability of specific protocols in various programming languages in *Chapter 5, Generating and Running Code in Different Languages*.

 As with transports, also when choosing protocol, you should go with the most popular (one of these three), unless you want some special functionality and know that it is implemented in your programming languages.

Processor

Processor is generated by the Apache Thrift compiler from your interface description document, so you don't have much choice here. It reads data from the input protocol, passes it to the handler, and sends the result to the output protocol. (Normally, both input and output protocols are the same.)

Server and client

The server combines all of the previously mentioned layers; it creates the transport, input, and output protocols (most of the time it is the same) processor based on the generated code, and protocols. Then it runs and waits for the incoming connections on the specified port.

In the simplest example, as the one in the previous chapter, you can use PHP and `TPhpStream` transport. In such case, you don't have to use Apache Thrift's server as you use the server that runs your PHP scripts.

Besides that, you can use any of the servers implemented with Apache Thrift. As with transports and protocols, there is a wide variety, and every programming language has a different choice. You can select any server you like the best for your solution. The most popular are:

- `TNonblockingServer`: This is a multithreaded, non-blocking I/O server that is optimized for handling concurrent connections.

- `TThreadPoolServer`: This is a multithreaded, blocking I/O server that uses much more resources than the previous one, but offers a better throughput.

- `TSimpleServer`: This is mainly used for testing purposes. It is single threaded with blocking I/O, which means it can process only one connection at a time.

You will learn how to use different (more advanced) servers in *Chapter 5, Generating and Running Code in Different Languages*.

Example

You may see the example of how the network stacks works in the excerpt from the PHP code from the previous chapter:

```php
$handler = new MyFirstHandler();
$processor = new \myfirst\MyFirstServiceProcessor($handler);


$transport = new TBufferedTransport(new TPhpStream(TPhpStream::MODE_R |
TPhpStream::MODE_W));
$protocol = new TBinaryProtocol($transport, true, true);


$transport->open();
$processor->process($protocol, $protocol);
$transport->close();
```

`handler` is implemented by the developer and as the name states, it is used to handle the service. Transport is chosen and passed to the `protocol` object. `processor` reads the data from the `protocol`, passes it to `handler`, and writes the result to the same protocol (thus the parameter `$protocol` is doubled).

In this case, the server is the whole file containing the preceding excerpt, as the `TPhpStream` transport is used. It allows reading and writing directly to the stream, so no intermediary is needed.

Apache Thrift's type system

Apache Thrift offers its own type system, which is designed to allow the developers to use the variable types native to their language of choice. Then, Thrift's libraries take care of translating the types between different languages.

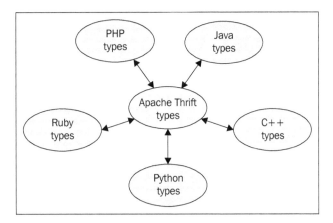

Apache Thrift creators divided its types into a few categories:

- **Basic**: These are the simplest types present in virtually every programming language.
- **Special**: These are those which don't fit into the basic category (currently, it is only one type).
- **Structs**: These are the equivalent of structs or classes from popular programming languages (with some limitations).
- **Container**: These are equivalent to commonly used container types in most of the programming languages.
- **Exceptions**: These are used to handle the errors.
- **Services**: These are core concept in Apache Thrift. They gather all the other types mentioned earlier to describe the procedures that can be called remotely. Exposing services is the main purpose of Apache Thrift.

IDL is a way of defining Apache Thrift types to create the services.

In this section, we will go through the Apache Thrift's types, getting to know how to construct the building blocks of the interface definition file structure.

Basic types

Basic variable types reflect those present in every programming language. Those are basic numeric, string and binary types:

- `bool`: Boolean value—`true` or `false`
- `byte`: Byte or 8-bit signed integer
- `i16`: 16-bit signed integer
- `i32`: 32-bit signed integer
- `i64`: 64-bit signed integer
- `double`: 64-bit double precision signed floating point number
- `string`: UTF-8 encoded text

Variable declarations don't appear by themselves in the interface description file; they are present in the service declaration, as a function attribute or in `typedef` statements.

In a function declaration, the type of the variable precedes its name, for example:

```
i32 add(1: i32number1, 2: i32number2)
```

The integer type names seem a little bit less readable in comparison to other languages, so the developers often tend to re-declare their name to create some more familiar name using the `typedef` statement:

```
typedefi32int
```

There are no unsigned integers as they are not implemented in many programming languages.

Special types

Currently, there is only one type of variable in the Apache Thrift's special types, and its developers plan to move it to the basic types at some point. It is a binary type, and it is a special case of string type. It offers the best interoperability and correctness when transmitting the binary data.

Structs

A `struct` is an object with a set of strongly typed fields, which is used to encapsulate similar variables. Some readers may immediately notice the similarity to C's structs.

Let's have a look at a simple `struct` in a very popular example:

```
struct Person {
1: required string first_name,
2: optional string middle_name,
3: required string last_name,
    4: i32 age = 0
}
```

As with many other syntax elements in Apache Thrift's IDL, the attributes are numbered. It is needed to preserve the compatibility between different versions of the services, you should keep the number with the corresponding attribute once and for all. More on the subject of versioning will be covered in *Chapter 8, Advanced Usage of Apache Thrift*. This identifier is positive, should be unique, but the numbers don't have to be consecutive.

You may mark the field as being `required` or `optional`. As the names state, the former will enforce you to a set given value, while the latter (which is default) will allow you to skip this field. Setting the required field may run you into trouble if you decide later on to remove this requirement (or the field altogether), but still have some instances of your application running the old version of the service.

You may also set the default value of the field, which will be used if you don't explicitly set this field's value.

One of the features of `struct` is that it can contain other `struct`:

```
struct Employee {
    1: i32id,
    2: Person person,
    3: string position
}
```

This way, you can construct more complex structures and since `struct` doesn't support inheritance, this syntax provides some kind of substitute.

Unions

Unions in Apache Thrift are similar to those in C and C++. They provide a set of possible fields of different types, and only one of them can be used. The syntax is the same as that for `struct` with the difference of using the `union` keyword instead of `struct`. Union's fields can't be set as required as any of the types is equally valid.

Let's look at the example definition of `union`:

```
unionMyNumber {
    1: i32number_int,
    2: string number_word
}
```

We defined `MyNumber` union, which can have either a 32-bit unsigned integer or string as a value, not both. So this function may take either of the variable types as a parameter:

```
void save_number(1: MyNumber number)
```

You can use any valid Apache Thrift data type in `union`.

Note that not all of the programming language support `union`. In such situations, there is a fallback to `struct`.

Containers

Apache Thrift's containers are mapped to the commonly available container types in the popular programming languages. They are strongly typed, which means that the types of keys and values are predefined. This may come as an inconvenience for programmers used to weakly typed languages, but is necessary to offer interoperability with strongly typed ones.

There are three types of containers with the syntax borrowed from the Java generics style.

list

`list` contains elements of a specified type. It is ordered and may contain duplicates. The syntax for `list` is:

```
list<type>
```

In the place of the `type` keyword, there should be an identifier of the type of the elements of `list`. For example, `list<i32>` is a list of 32-bit signed integers.

`list` is mapped to native lists or arrays in most of the programming languages, STL vector in C++, and `ArrayList` in Java.

set

`set` also contains elements of a specified type, but they are in contrast to `list`, unordered and unique (that means there are no duplicates allowed). The syntax for `set` is:

```
set<type>
```

As with `list`, in the place of the `type` keyword, there should be an identifier of the type of the elements of `set`. For example, `set<string>` is a set of strings.

`set` is mapped to the relevant set types. Set in Python, STL set in C++, `HashSet` in Java. In PHP, there are no sets, so Apache Thrift's sets are treated in the same way as lists.

map

`map` contains mapping of keys to values. The keys are strictly unique (that is, there couldn't be two values with the same key). The syntax for `map` is:

```
map<type1,type2>
```

As with other container types in the place of `type1` and `type2` keywords, there should be identifiers of the types of keys (former) and values (latter) of the map, for example, `map<i32,string>` is a map of unique 32-bit signed integers to strings.

Map is translated to an associative array in PHP, dictionary in Ruby and Python, STL map in C++, and HashMap in Java.

While any valid Apache Thrift type may be a key for the map, due to the restrictions of some programming languages that don't support more complex types as map keys, it is recommended that only basic types be used as keys. Moreover, when using JSON protocol, it is required that the keys are of basic type.

Usage of containers

Elements of sets can be of any valid Apache Thrift type.

Containers are used as any other type of variable. For example, `struct` that among other fields contains a list of strings — `list<string>` — is defined as:

```
struct Company {
    1: i32 id,
    2: string name,
    3: list<string> offices
}
```

A function that takes a list of integers list<i32> as an argument and returns a set of integers set<i32>, is declared in a service as:

```
set<i32> flatten(1: list<i32>mylist);
```

To make the code more concise, you may of course use containers with the typedef statement:

```
typedef map<i32,string>MyMap
```

Enums

Enum (enumerated type) is a data type that consists of a set of named values. The set cannot be modified. Its elements have values; they are assigned sequentially starting with 0, but you can set your own values. Let's have a look at the example:

```
enum Position {
CEO,
    MANAGER,
    SPECIALIST,
    TRAINEE = 9
}
```

In this example, the enumerated type Position consists of four values. They are written in uppercase, but it is a popular convention, not a syntax requirement. Everywhere you need, the values have to be referred by their full name, that is, Position.MANAGER.

Enums can be used as any other valid Apache Thrift data type, that is, as a parameter or a return value of functions:

```
Position getEmployeePosition(1: i32employee_id)
```

They also can be used in containers, for example, in list:

```
list<Position>getFreePositions()
```

It is also possible to add them to structs:

```
struct Employee {
    1: i32 id,
    2: Person person,
    3: Position position
}
```

Exceptions

Exceptions are similar to structs, with one difference that they are declared using the `exception` keyword. In Apache Thrift's implementation, in every programming language, they inherit from the native exception class thus integrating with the native exception handling.

In the interface definition file, exceptions are declared as follows:

```
exceptionMyError {
    1: i32 code,
    2: string message
}

exception WrongIdsError {
    1: string message,
    2: set<i32> ids  // list of unaccepted IDs
}
```

In this case, the `MyError` exception has a field for numeric error code and a message. `WrongIdsError` is more complex as it has a field that is a set of signed 32-bit integers. Any valid Apache Thrift type can be used in an exception.

As in Java, Apache Thrift needs you to declare the exceptions that we expect to be thrown by the function:

```
set<i32>findRecords(1: set<i32> ids) throws (1: MyErrorerror1, 2:
WrongIdsErrorerror2)
```

In this case, the `findRecords` function may throw `MyError` or `WrongIdsError` exceptions depending on the function's logic.

Services

This is where all Apache Thrift's type system components are combined to serve its main purpose: define the services that will be accessible from other applications. The `thrift` command (Apache Thrift's compiler) will parse the service definition and generate client and server stubs, which need to be implemented by the developer, like you did in *Chapter 3, Running Your First Apache Thrift Service and Client*.

The service's syntax is familiar to those who program in modern object-oriented programming languages; it looks almost exactly like the interface. The service consists of a set of function declarations, each with its parameters, return types, and optional information about thrown exceptions. It is also possible to declare the function as `oneway`, which means that the code will not wait for the response (thus, the function has to have `void` return type).

Services can extend other services. This simple inheritance model means that the child service will include its parent's function definitions.

Let's have a look at the example:

```
service PeopleDirectory {

    oneway void log(1: string message),
    void reloadDatabase()
}


service EmployeeDirectory extends PeopleDirectory {

    Employee findEmployee(1: i32employee_id) throws (1: MyError
error),
    bool createEmployee(1: Employee new_employee)
}
```

At the beginning, we have a service named `PeopleDirectory`, which may be some base service for the `people` directory. It has a function `log`:

```
oneway void log(1: string message)
```

It takes one argument (`message`) that when the function is implemented, we may presume will be saved to some logging backend, such as a file or a database. Note that this function is one way, which means that the program won't wait for the result; it is a quite common scenario in a case where a lot of information is being logged to the file. If we will not wait for the result, we can't expect the function to provide any; thus its return value type is `void`.

Such a service may be working standalone, but it also may be used in some other services, which we want to have something similar. In our example, the `EmployeeDirectory` service extends `PeopleDirectory` service, which means it exposes the `log` and `reloadDatabase` functions of `PeopleDirectory` along with its own set of functions. It's a typical inheritance model in object-oriented programming languages, which is implemented using the `extends` keyword:

```
serviceEmployeeDirectory extends PeopleDirectory {
```

Then, we have a declaration of different functions exposed by this service:

```
Employee findEmployee(1: i32employee_id) throws (1: MyError error),
    bool createEmployee(1: Employee new_employee)
```

The functions, similar to those in C++ or Java can take as an argument and return a value of any valid Apache Thrift type (including `void`). They can also throw an exception (or more than one).

Note that in Apache Thrift, you can extend only one service at a time; there is no multiple inheritance.

IDL syntax

Now that you have the knowledge of the Apache Thrift's variable types, it is time to put those together in a single file describing our interface.

 In this section, only the most important elements of official IDL syntax were described. If you would like to go deeper into the details, read the formal syntax definition or learn about deprecated elements at https://thrift.apache.org/docs/idl.

Apache Thrift's IDL syntax will be familiar to the developers programming in C++, Java, or even PHP. Let's have a look at the most important components.

Comments

Apache Thrift supports three types of comments. The first is a bash-style comment—a line beginning with #:

```
# This is a comment
```

The second syntax is C++/Java/PHP-style—a line with // at the beginning:

```
// This is a comment
```

The last type of supported comment syntax is C-style multiline with /* at the beginning and */ at the end (using space and * at the beginning of every line is a common convention in many programming languages, although it is not required):

```
/*
 * This is C-style
 * multiline
 * comment.
 */
```

It can also be used as a one line comment:

```
/* this is one line C-style comment */
```

Of course, it is up to you which style you will use; they are perfectly equivalent.

Comments can be used anywhere in your IDL file and they are ignored when the document is parsed.

Document

The formal name for your Apache Thrift IDL file (that is, `myfirst.thrift`) is **document**. Anything that is inside this file is either a header or a definition. Any document can contain 0 or more headers and definitions. It may sound weird, but after reading this section, you will be able to easily identify every part of your document.

Headers

Headers are statements that don't define any objects that can be used in the document, or in the services. They contain special instructions regarding the processing of the file or generating the service stubs.

There are three types of headers that we will review:

- Thrift include
- C++ include
- Namespace

Let's start with the first one.

Thrift include

This is Apache Thrift's `include`; it looks like this:

```
include "shared.thrift"
```

This syntax is very common in other programming languages. Apache Thrift compiler will read those files and include any definitions present in this file (structs, services, and so on). Provided files are searched in the current path or by searching in any paths provided in the `-I` flag to the compiler, for example, if you have some special Thrift files that you want to use through different projects in the `~/includes` directory, you should use following command to be sure that they are found and included:

```
$ thrift --gen php -I ~/includes myfirst.thrift
```

Objects included in such a way are accessed using the name of the file as a prefix to their name, so for example, if you have included the file `shared.thrift` and in this file there was `structmystruct`, you can access it with `shared.mystruct`.

C++ include

This is a special keyword used when you specifically want to have some extra `include` in your C++ code generated from this document.

So, for example, if you want to have the following `include` statement in your C++ code generated by the Thrift compiler:

```
#include <vector>
```

You have to use the following header in your Apache Thrift document:

```
cpp_include "<vector>"
```

Namespace

Various programming languages have different methods of categorizing and separating the files related to different logic; such separated units are often called packages, modules, or namespaces. They are called **uniformly namespaces** in Apache Thrift documents. By setting a proper namespace, you order thrift compiler to place the code generated for a given language, in a desired place.

Namespaces are defined per programming language and can be different for each of them:

```
namespace java myfirst
namespace phpmyfirstthrift
namespace rb mf
```

Of course, for the sake of simplicity and to avoid mistakes, it is better to have the same namespace for every language using * in place of the language identifier:

```
namespace * myfirst
```

Every Apache Thrift document is compiled to the desired namespace; it applies to the included documents too.

> There are some extra namespace rules for Smalltalk. If you plan to use this programming language, refer to the Apache Thrift documentation at https://thrift.apache.org/docs/idl.

Definitions

Definition is the other type of element present in the Apache Thrift document. In short, everything that is neither `include` (Thrift or C++) or `namespace` command is a definition. In the document, various building blocks are defined to reach the ultimate purpose, which is defining the service.

In the Apache Thrift document, you can define:

- const
- typedef
- enum
- struct
- union
- exception
- service

Those of the definitions that are Apache Thrift's data types were described in the previous section, so here we are going to concentrate only on const and typedef, which were not mentioned earlier.

const

The const keyword is used to define the constant value. This value can then be used in other definitions in the document. The purpose of this element is to have one place when some constant value is defined, instead of having it set in different places of the file. The value may change during the development (that is, for testing purposes) but will not change after the code is generated. Common usage for such language construct is to define some physical or mathematical value, for example:

```
const double PI = 3.1415926
```

In this example, const is followed by the type name (double), const name (PI), and the value (3.1415926).

The values of the complex types and structs are defined using JSON notation, for example, constant, which is a map, is declared in the following way:

```
const map<i32,string> CITIES = {0: "New York", 1: "London", 2: "Madrid"}
```

List constant:

```
const list<string> LANGUAGES = ["PHP", "Java", "C++"]
```

It is also possible to set const of previously defined struct, for example:

```
struct city {
    1: string name,
    2: i32 population
}

const city NEW_YORK = {"name": "New York", "population": 8500000}
```

As you see any valid Apache Thrift type can be used to declare `const` and there are a lot of possible combinations.

typedef

The `typedef` keyword is used to give other names to the Apache Thrift type. The commonly used case is renaming the integer type names `i16`, `i32`, and `i64`, for example:

```
typedef i32 integer
typedef i32 myinteger
typedef i64 userid
```

In this case, `integer` or `myinteger` can be used instead of `i32` and `userid` instead of `i64`. The same Apache Thrift type can be mapped to many different names.

It is also common to give pretty names to the complex types so that they are easier to handle, for example:

```
typedef map<i32,string> EmployeeList
```

In this case, `map` mapping unique 32-bit unsigned integers to strings becomes the `EmployeeList` type.

Summary

In this chapter, you learned a lot of new information. First, you saw how the Apache Thrift looks from the developer's perspective; you got the tool necessary to work. If you were curious enough, you got deep into the technical details to know the network stack, including some of the transports, protocols, and servers.

Then, you got to know Apache Thrift's data types and other elements of IDL—building blocks of your services.

Having this foundation, you are ready to go deeper into the implementation of Apache Thrift in various programming languages. In fact, you are able now to design and develop your own advanced services. In the next chapter, we will work on strengthening these skills.

5
Generating and Running Code in Different Languages

In the previous chapter, we ran through the internals of Apache Thrift, to give you the skills needed to design your own services. By now you should be able to define your interface description file, compile it with Thrift tool, run the server and launch the client. You also saw how the code looks like in two popular programming languages (PHP and Python).

Now, we will dive even deeper, looking into the code that Apache Thrift generates, but also covering a broader spectrum of programming languages. At the time of writing, there are libraries for 23 languages in the Apache Thrift code repository. Here, I will cover six of the most popular ones:

- PHP
- Java
- Python
- JavaScript
- Ruby
- C++

Each language will be covered separately, so to understand the subsection about your language of choice, you don't have to read about those you are not interested in. However, I suggest at least skimming over all of them, to grasp the power of Apache Thrift and see how the same concept is tackled differently.

In this chapter, the following topics will be covered for each of the programming languages:

- Compiler options for this language
- Examination of generated code
- Available transports, protocols, and servers
- Creating and running the server and client

We will be working on a slightly modified code that you know from *Chapter 3, Running Your First Apache Thrift Service and Client*. For your convenience, you can download it from Packt's website with the code for every language already generated. So you can examine it, even if you don't have the Apache Thrift compiler installed and configured. There are some small changes. First, we substituted `namespace` for PHP and Python with more general syntax for every language:

```
namespace php myfirst
namespace py myfirst
```

So instead of the preceding code, we have the following:

```
namespace * myfirst
```

Second, there are some extra declarations covering all of the available variable types (as of Apache Thrift 0.9.2). You won't use them, but after compilation you can examine the files to see how such variables are handled. Here's the extra code:

```
struct MyStruct {
    1: bool mybool,
    2: byte mybyte,
    3: i16 myi16,
    4: i32 myi32,
    5: i64 myi64,
    6: double mydouble,
    7: string mystring,
    8: list<i32> mylist,
    9: set<i32> myset,
    10: map<i32,i32> mymap
}

union MyUnion {
    1: bool mybool,
    2: string mystring
}

enum MyEnum {
```

```
        ENUM1,
        ENUM2,
        ENUM3
}

exception MyError {
    1: int error_code,
    2: string error_description
}
```

This way we have all of them covered. Just to be sure, the full code looks like this:

```
// namespaces are used in resulting packages
namespace * myfirst

const double PI = 3.1415926

struct MyStruct {
    1: bool mybool,
    2: byte mybyte,
    3: i16 myi16,
    4: i32 myi32,
    5: i64 myi64,
    6: double mydouble,
    7: string mystring,
    8: list<i32> mylist,
    9: set<i32> myset,
    10: map<i32,i32> mymap
}

union MyUnion {
    1: bool mybool,
    2: string mystring
}

enum MyEnum {
    ENUM1,
    ENUM2,
    ENUM3
}

exception MyError {
    1: int error_code,
    2: string error_description
}
```

```
typedef i32 int

// here starts the service definition
service MyFirstService {

    // log method - it saves timestamp to given file
    oneway void log(1:string filename),

    // multiply method - returns result of multiplication of two
integers; it returns integer as well
    int multiply(1:int number1, 2:int number2),

    // get_log_size method returns the size of the log file; throws an
exception when problems occur
    int get_log_size(1:string filename) throws (1:MyError error),

}
```

So, let's get started with PHP.

PHP

PHP is one of the most popular programming languages used mainly for server-side scripting of web applications (however, it may be used also as a general purpose language). It is relatively easy to learn and simple to use with thousands of popular applications written in it.

Generating the code

Apache Thrift's compiler offers a bunch of options for PHP. Run the following command to see them:

```
$ thrift --help
```

Look for the information about PHP generators given below:

```
php (PHP):
    inlined:           Generate PHP inlined files
    server:            Generate PHP server stubs
    oop:               Generate PHP with object oriented subclasses
    rest:              Generate PHP REST processors
    nsglobal=NAME:     Set global namespace
    validate:          Generate PHP validator methods
    json:              Generate JsonSerializable classes (requires PHP >=
5.4)
```

Some of the options may cater to your project's specific needs. Their descriptions may be cryptic, so here's some extra explanation:

- `inlined`: The data encoding is done inline in the generated PHP file.
- `oop`: The generated code is somewhat more object-oriented. With classes extending `TBase`, it is mutually exclusive with inlined.
- `server`: This adds a service processor, which is required to run the service (you don't need it if you want to implement PHP only in the client).
- `rest`: Some extra parameter processing is added, so the received values are casted at the proper types.
- `validate`: Extra validation is added; so if the received value is null, an exception is thrown.
- `nsglobal=NAME`: An extra namespace is added at the top of the already defined namespaces.
- `json`: The generated classes implement PHP's `JsonSerializable` interface present in PHP >= 5.4 (read more on `http://php.net/manual/en/class.jsonserializable.php`).

You need to pick the options from the list to match your project's needs. It is possible to use more than one, for example, if you would like your code to not only be `JsonSerializable`, but also contain a service class, run the following command:

```
$ thrift --gen php:json,server myfirst.thrift
```

 Be aware that you won't get any error message if you misspell the parameter, it will just be ignored. It's hard to debug such a situation, so just check your parameters twice.

Examining the code

The code that you generated will be in the `gen-php` directory (or, if you chose the `inlined` option, then in the `gen-phpi` directory). Inside the directory, there will be a namespace structure (if you chose any) containing the PHP files for each of the services that you declared. Separately, there is the `Types.php` file, which contains the variables generated from your definition.

Let's have a look at this file. As PHP is dynamically typed, the types of variables are really a matter of convention and adding extra checking when reading or writing. As a result, the simple structure becomes an elaborate class with various methods handling the variables.

Now, let's have a look at the `MyFirstService.php` file. It contains the `MyFirstServiceIf` interface:

```
interface MyFirstServiceIf {
  /**
   * @param string $filename
   */
  public function log($filename);
  /**
   * @param int $number1
   * @param int $number2
   * @return int
   */
  public function multiply($number1, $number2);
  /**
   * @param string $filename
   * @return int
   * @throws \myfirst\MyError
   */
  public function get_log_size($filename);
}
```

In object-oriented programming, an interface is a description of the elements that the class that implements it has to have. Therefore, you need to implement all of the methods of your interface for the service to exist; in this case the `log`, `multiply`, and `get_log_size` methods you declared in your Apache Thrift document. There are annotations that will suggest you the behavior of the service.

Another important element in the `MyFirstService.php` file is the `MyFirstServiceClient` class. This class implements the service's interface as well, with the purpose of exposing public methods that you can use in your client script.

If you chose the server compiler option, you will also have the `MyFirstServiceProcessor` class generated. This is the processor that is needed to run the server for your service.

Transports

PHP implementation of Apache Thrift offers a variety of transports. You can always look them up in the `lib/php/lib/Thrift/Transport`. There are all of the most popular transports described in *Chapter 4, Understanding How Apache Thrift Works*, excluding file transport, which is not available in PHP.

One transport specific for PHP is `TPhpStream`, which reads from and writes to PHP's standard streams `php://input` and `php://output`. In this way, you don't need to run your own server to provide the service; you can use an existing HTTP server such as nginx or Apache HTTP Server.

If you intend to use one of the transports, I suggest you examine the implementation to be sure how it works and if it fits your specific needs.

Protocols

PHP implementation of Apache Thrift offers all of the standard protocols mentioned in *Chapter 4*, *Understanding How Apache Thrift Works*. Additionally, it provides `TMultiplexedProtocol`, which is not a standalone protocol, but a decorator that helps you deal with complex scenarios when you want to use multiple services on one server (called **multiplexing**).

Implementations of the protocols are in the `lib/php/lib/Thrift/Protocol` directory where you can examine them before using.

Servers

In PHP, there are the implementations of `TSimpleServer` and `TForkingServer`. Additionally, you can use any HTTP server already running by using the TPhpStream transport.

Implementations of the servers are relatively simple and you can examine them in the `lib/php/lib/Thrift/Server` directory.

Implementing and running the service

Implementing the service is done by creating a handler implementing the interface that was generated by Apache Thrift; in our case, it is `MyFirstServiceIf`. The methods should accept and return the variables of the declared types.

The source code below indicates how to do it. For the sake of brevity, the implementation details of the methods were omitted:

```php
#!/usr/bin/env php
<?php

# path to your Apache Thrift library
define('THRIFT_PHP_LIB', __DIR__ .'/thrift-0.9.2/lib/php/lib');
# path to the files generated by the Apache Thrift compiler
```

```php
define('GEN_PHP_DIR', __DIR__.'/gen-php');

require_once THRIFT_PHP_LIB.'/Thrift/ClassLoader/ThriftClassLoader.
php';

use Thrift\ClassLoader\ThriftClassLoader;

$loader = new ThriftClassLoader();
$loader->registerNamespace('Thrift', THRIFT_PHP_LIB);
// register your namespace
$loader->registerDefinition('myfirst', GEN_PHP_DIR);
$loader->register();

// include here the protocols and transports that you need
use Thrift\Protocol\TBinaryProtocol;
use Thrift\Transport\TPhpStream;
use Thrift\Transport\TBufferedTransport;

// implementing the service interface
class MyFirstHandler implements \myfirst\MyFirstServiceIf {

    public function log($filename) {
        // implementation of log function
    }

    public function multiply($number1, $number2) {
        // implementation of multiply function
    }


    public function get_log_size($filename) {
        // implementation of get_log_size function
    }

};

header('Content-Type', 'application/x-thrift');
echo "\r\n";

// instantiation of our handler
$handler = new MyFirstHandler();

$processor = new \myfirst\MyFirstServiceProcessor($handler);
```

```php
$transport = new TBufferedTransport(new TPhpStream(TPhpStream::MODE_R
| TPhpStream::MODE_W));
$protocol = new TBinaryProtocol($transport, true, true);

$transport->open();
$processor->process($protocol, $protocol);
$transport->close();
```

In this case, the service is run through the other already installed HTTP server. Save this code to the file (for example, `MyFirstServer.php`), upload it to the server, and point any clients to the address representing this file.

Implementing and running the client

To run the client using the PHP Apache Thrift implementation, you need to prepare the environment in the same manner as with a server. Then, you can call your remote procedures using the instance of your service's client, which was generated by the compiler; in our case, it is `MyFirstServiceClient`. Let's have a look at the example:

```php
#!/usr/bin/env php
<?php

# path to your Apache Thrift library
define('THRIFT_PHP_LIB', __DIR__.'/thrift-0.9.2/lib/php/lib');
# path to the files generated by the Apache Thrift compiler
define('GEN_PHP_DIR', __DIR__.'/gen-php');

require_once THRIFT_PHP_LIB.'/Thrift/ClassLoader/ThriftClassLoader.
php';

use Thrift\ClassLoader\ThriftClassLoader;

$loader = new ThriftClassLoader();
$loader->registerNamespace('Thrift', THRIFT_PHP_LIB);
// register your namespace
$loader->registerDefinition('myfirst', GEN_PHP_DIR);
$loader->register();

// include here the protocols and transports that you need
use Thrift\Protocol\TBinaryProtocol;
use Thrift\Transport\TSocket;
use Thrift\Transport\THttpClient;
use Thrift\Transport\TBufferedTransport;
use Thrift\Exception\TException;
```

```
// provide hostname, port number and URL of your service
$server = new THttpClient('localhost', 8080, '/MyFirstServiceServer.
php');

// create connection
$transport = new TBufferedTransport($server, 1024, 1024);
$protocol = new TBinaryProtocol($transport);
$client = new \myfirst\MyFirstServiceClient($protocol);

$transport->open();

// run remote methods with $client->methodname($param)
$client->log('lofgile.log');
print $client->multiply(2,21);

$transport->close();
```

If you want to use the custom variable types defined by you, that is, our `MyStruct` struct, you can instantiate it with:

```
$ms = new \myfirst\MyStruct();
```

Then work with it as with any other class to read or write values, for example:

```
$ms->myi32 = 42;
print $ms->myi32;
```

Save your client code to the file, `MyFirstClient.php`, and simply run the PHP file from the command line:

```
php -f MyFirstClient.php
```

Of course, you can also embed the client code in your application, depending on your needs.

Java

Java is another programming language, which is extremely popular these days. Used not only for desktop applications, but also in the web applications in the embedded devices or on the mobile phones and tablets (Android being a notable case), Apache Thrift is used in all of those scenarios.

Generating the code

Apache Thrift's compiler offers lots of options for Java. Run the following command to see them:

```
$ thrift --help
```

Look for the information about Java generators:

```
java (Java):
    beans:              Members will be private, and setter methods will
return void.
    private-members: Members will be private, but setter methods will
return 'this' like usual.
    nocamel:            Do not use CamelCase field accessors with beans.
    fullcamel:          Convert underscored_accessor_or_service_names to
camelCase.
    android:            Generated structures are Parcelable.
    android_legacy:  Do not use java.io.IOException(throwable) (available
for Android 2.3 and above).
    java5:              Generate Java 1.5 compliant code (includes android_
legacy flag).
    reuse-objects:   Data objects will not be allocated, but existing
instances will be used (read and write).
    sorted_containers:
                        Use TreeSet/TreeMap instead of HashSet/HashMap as an
implementation of set/map.
```

Some of the options may cater to your project's specific needs and they are self-explanatory.

You need to pick the options from the list to match your project's needs. It is possible to use more than one, for example, if you would like your code to have private members and have the structures parsable, use:

```
$ thrift --gen java:private-members,android myfirst.thrift
```

Be aware that you won't get any error message if you misspell the parameter; it will just be ignored. It's hard to debug such a situation, so just check your parameters twice.

Examining the code

The code that you have generated will be in the gen-java directory, or if you chose the beans option, then in the gen-javabean directory. Inside the directory, there will be a namespace structure (if you chose any) containing the Java files for each of the complex variable types (such as structs, exceptions, enums, and so on), constants, and services that you declared.

You can examine the files containing the variables and constants to see an elaborate implementation of the behavior intended by Apache Thrift.

Now, let's have a look at the service file which, in the case of our example, is MyFirstService.java. It contains the MyFirstService class. This class contains other important interfaces and classes, notably the Iface interface:

```
public interface Iface {

  public void log(String filename) throws org.apache.thrift.
TException;

  public int multiply(int number1, int number2) throws org.apache.
thrift.TException;

  public int get_log_size(String filename) throws MyError, org.apache.
thrift.TException;

}
```

An interface is a description of the elements that the class which extends it has to have. Therefore, you need to implement all of the methods of your interface for the service to exist; in this case the log, multiply, and get_log_size methods you declared in your Apache Thrift document.

The MyFirstService class also contains the Client subclass, which implements the Iface interface which you will use in your client application.

Transports

There are a lot of transports available in the Java implementation of Apache Thrift. You can look them up in the lib/java/src/org/apache/thrift/transport directory. There are all of the most popular transports described in *Chapter 4, Understanding How Apache Thrift Works*.

There are also a few nonstandard transports that you may find particularly useful. They are:

- `TFastFramedTransport`: This transport is compatible with `TFramedTransport`, but offers some optimizations which are beneficial in terms of memory usage, when your messages are of more-or-less similar size.

- `TSaslClientTransport` and `TSaslServerTransport`: Those are layered transports for client and server that are used if you need to provide security through the **Simple Authentication and Security Layer** (**SASL**) framework.

If you intend to use one of the transports, I suggest you examine the implementation to be sure how it works and if it fits your specific needs.

Protocols

In addition to the standard protocols, which were discussed in *Chapter 4, Understanding How Apache Thrift Works*, Java implementation of Apache Thrift offers `TMultiplexedProtocol`, which is a decorator that helps you deal with multiplexing—multiple services on one server.

Implementations of the protocols are in the `lib/java/src/org/apache/thrift/protocol` directory, where you can examine them before using them.

Servers

The Java implementation of Apache Thrift offers all of the basic servers mentioned in *Chapter 4, Understanding How Apache Thrift Works*. Additionally, there are some other servers that you might find useful.

The first of them is `TThreadPoolServer`, which uses Java's Thread Pools to manage the workers.

Two others are implementing the Half-Sync/Half-Async architectural pattern to provide concurrent I/O, which combines asynchronous handling of connections with synchronous processing of the following requests:

- `THsHaServer`: This is an extension of `TNonblockingServer`.

- `TThreadedSelectorServer`: This performs better than `THsHaServer` in multicore environments.

You can examine the implementations of the servers in the `lib/java/src/org/apache/thrift/server` directory.

Implementing and running the service

Implementing the service is done by creating a handler class, which implements the interface that was generated by Apache Thrift; in our case, it is `MyFirstService.Iface`. Then the server needs to be created.

The following source code indicates how to perform the first step. For brevity, the implementation details of the methods were omitted:

```
import org.apache.thrift.TException;

// import code generated by Apache Thrift compiler
import myfirst.*;

public class MyFirstHandler implements MyFirstService.Iface {

    public MyFirstHandler() {
    }


    public void log(String filename) {
        // implementation omitted
    }

    public int multiply(int number1, int number2) {
        // implementation omitted
    }

    public int get_log_size(String filename) {
        // implementation omitted
    }

}
```

Let's save this handler to a file, that is, `MyFirstHandler.java`.

The second part is to create the server:

```
import org.apache.thrift.server.TServer;
import org.apache.thrift.server.TServer.Args;
import org.apache.thrift.server.TThreadPoolServer;
import org.apache.thrift.transport.TServerSocket;
import org.apache.thrift.transport.TServerTransport;

// import code generated by Apache Thrift compiler
```

```
import myfirst.*;

public class MyFirstServer {

    public static MyFirstHandler handler;

    public static MyFirstService.Processor processor;

    public static void myserver(MyFirstService.Processor processor) {
        TServerTransport serverTransport = new TServerSocket(8080);
        TServer server = new TThreadPoolServer(new TThreadPoolServer.
Args(serverTransport).processor(processor));
        server.serve();
    }

    // main function
    public static void main(String [] args) {
        handler = new MyFirstHandler();
        processor = new MyFirstService.Processor(handler);

        Runnable server = new Runnable() {
            public void run() {
                myserver(processor);
            }
        };

        new Thread(server).start();
    }

}
```

Save it to the file, for example, `MyFirstServer.java`. Now, you can compile the code and run the server:

```
$ javac MyFirstServer.java
$ java MyFirstServer
```

Implementing and running the client

Running the client using the Java implementation of Apache Thrift is easy: you need to create a proper environment (transport, protocol) and use the client (in our case `MyFirstService.Client`), which exposes the service's methods.

Here's the code example:

```
// Import code generated by Apache Thrift compiler
import myfirst.*;

import org.apache.thrift.transport.TTransport;
import org.apache.thrift.transport.TSocket;
import org.apache.thrift.protocol.TBinaryProtocol;
import org.apache.thrift.protocol.TProtocol;

public class MyFirstClient {
    public static void main(String [] args) {

        TTransport transport = new TSocket("localhost", 8080);
        transport.open();

        TProtocol protocol = new TBinaryProtocol(transport);
        MyFirstService.Client client = new MyFirstService.
Client(protocol);

        // call remote functions
        client.log("logfile.log");
        System.out.println(client.multiply(14,3));

        transport.close();
    }
}
```

You can embed your client's code in your application or just save it to the
`MyFirstClient.java` file, compile, and run:

```
$ javac MyFirstClient.java
$ java  MyFirstClient
```

Python

Python is used universally in server scripting, web and desktop applications,
networking, natural language processing, statistical analysis, machine learning, and
lots of other applications. This makes it a great tool for distributed applications with
strong support in Apache Thrift.

Generating the code

Apache Thrift's compiler offers lots of options for Python. Run the following command to see them:

```
$ thrift --help
```

Look for the information about Python generators:

```
  py (Python):
    new_style:        Generate new-style classes.
    twisted:          Generate Twisted-friendly RPC services.
    tornado:          Generate code for use with Tornado.
    utf8strings:      Encode/decode strings using utf8 in the generated
code.
    slots:            Generate code using slots for instance members.
    dynamic:          Generate dynamic code, less code generated but
slower.
    dynbase=CLS       Derive generated classes from class CLS instead of
TBase.
    dynexc=CLS        Derive generated exceptions from CLS instead of
TExceptionBase.
    dynimport='from foo.bar import CLS'
                      Add an import line to generated code to find the
dynbase class.
```

Some of the options may cater to your project's specific needs. Here's a brief explanation of the most important of them, which we will use:

- `new_style`: The classes will be generated in Python's "new style", which boils down to inheriting from the object (for more information about new style classes in Python, refer to the Python wiki: `https://wiki.python.org/moin/NewClassVsClassicClass`)

- `twisted`: The generated code will be compatible with the Twisted asynchronous networking framework (`https://twistedmatrix.com/`)

- `tornado`: The generated code will be compatible with the Tornado framework (`http://www.tornadoweb.org/`)

- `utf8strings`: It's an important option when developing applications in languages other than English that all the strings are properly encoded and decoded using the UTF-8 codec

- `slots`: Python's slots are used for instance members (see `https://docs.python.org/2/reference/datamodel.html#slots`) to save space when creating multiple objects

You need to pick the options from the list to match your project's needs. It is possible to use more than one, for example, if you need your code to have new style classes and have the strings encoded and decoded in UTF-8, run the following command:

```
$ thrift --gen py:new_style,utf8strings myfirst.thrift
```

Watch out, because you won't get any error message if you misspell the parameter; it will just will ignored. It's hard to debug such a situation, so just check your parameters twice.

Examining the code

The code that you generated will be in the following directory:

- `gen-py.twisted`: If you wanted to have the Twisted-compatible code (`twisted` option)
- `gen-py.tornado`: If you generated the Tornado-compatible code (`tornado` option)
- `gen-py`: In any other case

Inside the directory, there will be a namespace structure (if you chose any) containing two Python files for each of the services that you declared. Separately, there is a `ttypes.py` file, which contains the variables generated from your definition and a `constants.py` file, which contains all of the constants. You can note that while consts are defined very simply as a variable (there are no constants in Python), the variables are elaborate with a huge amount of code to handle them. Note that there are the __ init__.py files present, which make a module out of the code that was generated.

Let us have a look at the service files. In our example, the `MyFirstService.py` file contains the `Iface` class (because in Python there is no equivalent to interfaces known from other object-oriented programming languages):

```python
class Iface:
  def log(self, filename):
    """
    Parameters:
     - filename
    """
    pass

  def multiply(self, number1, number2):
    """
    Parameters:
     - number1
     - number2
    """
```

```
    pass

def get_log_size(self, filename):
    """
    Parameters:
     - filename
    """
    pass
```

In your implementation of the service, you are going to define all the methods, which currently do nothing (just pass); in this case the `log`, `multiply`, and `get_log_size` methods you declared in your Apache Thrift document. There are annotations that will suggest you what parameters the methods will take, however, contrary to the implementation for other languages, the suggestions for the types of parameters and return value are missing.

Another important element in the `MyFirstService.py` file is the `Client` class. You will use this class in your client script to call the service and run remote methods. In fact, the creators of the Python implementation went an extra step forward and have the compiler to generate a file with the service name suffixed with `-remote` (in our case, `MyFirstService-remote`). This script contains an implementation of the client; more on that later.

Transports

In addition to the most popular transports described in *Chapter 4, Understanding How Apache Thrift Works*, the Python implementation of Apache Thrift offers some other transports as well. You can look up the list in the code repository in the `lib/py/src/transport` directory. Some of the basic transports are the classes in the `TTransport.py` file, while the others are in separate files.

Some of the nonstandard transports you may find particularly useful are:

- `TMemoryBuffer`: The wrapper for the `StringIO` object, so you are able to write to or read from the memory; if you pass the value in the constructor it will be a transport for reading; otherwise, for writing

- `TSSLSocket`: Used for creating sockets wrapped in the SSL security layer

- `TSaslClient`: Similarly to in Java, this is a layered transport for the client which is used if you need to provide security through the SASL framework

- `TZlibTransport`: A layered transport that compresses the transport that it gets using Python's `zlib` library

- `THttpClient`: Implements `TTransportBase` to provide communication over HTTP or HTTPS

For THttpClient, use URI in the constructor:

```
THttpClient('http://host:port/path')
```

So, for example, if the server is running on the localhost, on port 8080 and its path is /MyFirstServer, the instantiation of the client class would be:

```
client = THttpClient('http://localhost:8080/MyFirstServer')
```

If you intend to use one of those transports, I suggest you examine the implementation to be sure how it works and if it fits your specific needs.

Protocols

Python implementation of Apache Thrift offers all of the standard protocols mentioned in *Chapter 4, Understanding How Apache Thrift Works*. Additionally, it provides TMultiplexedProtocol, which is not a standalone protocol, but a decorator that helps you deal with complex scenarios when you want to use multiple services on one server (called **multiplexing**).

Implementations of the protocols are in the lib/py/src/protocol directory, where you can examine them before using.

Servers

The Python implementation of Apache Thrift contains all of the popular servers that we mentioned in *Chapter 4, Understanding How Apache Thrift Works*. Moreover, it contains a few more, which you may find useful in certain scenarios:

- TThreadedServer: A threaded server that spawns a new thread for each connection

- TForkingServer: Forks a new process for each request, and is more scalable than TThreadedServer

- TProcessPoolServer: A server with a fixed pool of worker subprocesses to serve the requests

- THttpServer: A simple HTTP server, not very perfromant

You can examine the implementations of the servers in the lib/py/src/server directory of the Apache Thrift package. Some of the basic servers are the classes in the TServer.py file, while the others are in separate files.

Building the libraries

To run the Python code, we need to have the Apache Thrift libraries built. Instead of installing it system-wise, we can have them in the local copy.

Copy the archive that you downloaded from the Apache Thrift website to your project created directory and decompress it:

```
$ tar -xvzf thrift-0.9.2.tar.gz
```

Now, we will have full Apache Thrift in the `thrift-0.9.2` directory (the name may differ, depending on the version, substitute it in all commands). The Python libraries are in the `thrift-0.9.2/lib` directory and they need to be built. Enter the `thrift-0.9.2/lib/py` directory and run the `setup` command. This library will not be installed system-wise, but just built in place:

```
$ cd thrift-0.9.2/lib/py
$ python setup.py build
$ cd ../../..
```

Implementing and running the service

As in other languages, implementing the service is done by creating a handler that implements the interface that was generated by Apache Thrift; in our case, it is `MyFirstService.Iface`. The methods should accept and return the variables of declared types.

The following source code indicates how to do it. For brevity, the implementation details of the methods were omitted:

```python
import sys, glob

# path for file generated by Apache Thrift Compiler
sys.path.append('gen-py')
# add path where built Apache Thrift libraries are
sys.path.insert(0, glob.glob('thrift-0.9.2/lib/py/build/lib.*')[0])

from myfirst import MyFirstService
from myfirst.ttypes import *
from myfirst.constants import *

from thrift.transport import TSocket
from thrift.transport import TTransport
from thrift.protocol import TBinaryProtocol
```

```
from thrift.server import TServer

class MyFirstHandler(MyFirstService.Iface):
    def __init__(self):
        pass

    def log(self, filename):
        # implement log here
        pass

    def multiply(self, number1, number2):
        # implement multiply here
        pass

    def get_log_size(self, filename):
        # implement get_log_size here
        pass

handler = MyFirstHandler()
processor = MyFirstService.Processor(handler)
transport = TSocket.TServerSocket(port=8080)
tfactory = TTransport.TBufferedTransportFactory()
pfactory = TBinaryProtocol.TBinaryProtocolFactory()

server = TServer.TSimpleServer(processor, transport, tfactory,
pfactory)

server.serve()
```

To start the server, save this code to the `MyFirstServer.py` file and run the following command:

```
$ python MyFirstServer.py
```

Your server will be running on the localhost, port `8080`.

Implementing and running the client

As I mentioned earlier, the Apache Thrift compiler generates an example client script, which is in the file prefixed with -remote, in our case, `MyFirstService-remote`. This client runs out of the box and allows you to test your service. For example, to test the `multiply` method, you can run:

```
$ ./MyFirstService-remote multiply 7 6
```

To see the list of possible methods, run:

```
$ ./MyFirstService-remote --help
```

This script is a great resource to learn how the client code should be written.

To run the client using the PHP Apache Thrift implementation, you need to prepare the network stack. Then, after connecting, you can call your remote procedures using the instance of your service's client that was generated by the compiler; in our case, it is `MyFirstService.Client`. Let's have a look at the example code, which is very simple:

```
import sys, glob

# add path with Apache Thrift compiler generated files
sys.path.append('gen-py')
# add path where built Apache Thrift libraries are
sys.path.insert(0, glob.glob('thrift-0.9.2/lib/py/build/lib.*')[0])

from myfirst import MyFirstService
from myfirst.ttypes import *
from myfirst.constants import *

from thrift import Thrift
from thrift.transport import TSocket
from thrift.transport import TTransport
from thrift.protocol import TBinaryProtocol

transport = TSocket.TSocket('localhost', 8080)
transport = TTransport.TBufferedTransport(transport)
protocol = TBinaryProtocol.TBinaryProtocol(transport)
client = MyFirstService.Client(protocol)

transport.open()

client.log('logile.log')
print client.multiply(2,21)

transport.close()
```

If you want to use the variable types defined by you, that is, our `MyStruct` struct, it is very easy to instantiate them:

```
ms = MyStruct()
```

Then, work with it as with any other class to read or write values, for example:

```
ms.myi32 = 42
print ms.myi32
```

You can run your client by simply saving the code to the file, that is, `MyFirstClient.py` and running the Python file from the command line:

```
$ python MyFirstClient.py
```

Of course, you can also embed the client code in your application depending on your needs.

JavaScript

JavaScript is a scripting language used mainly for frontend development in web applications, but it has also gained popularity recently in server-side solutions with Node.js.

JavaScript code generated by the Apache Thrift compiler (Node.js aside) is strictly client-side, intended to be used in the web browser against the services written in other languages.

Generating the code

Apache Thrift's compiler offers few options for JavaScript. Run the following command to see them:

```
$ thrift --help
```

Look for the information about JavaScript generators:

```
js (Javascript):
  jquery:          Generate jQuery compatible code.
  node:            Generate node.js compatible code.
  ts:              Generate TypeScript definition files.
```

Running the generator without any options will provide you with just plain JavaScript code. Let's explain the extra options:

- `Jquery`: The generated code will be jQuery compatible
- `Node`: Code for Node.js will be generated; technically, this is still JavaScript code, however this is a completely different runtime environment, so we will won't discuss it here. If you use this option, your file will be created in the `gen-nodejs` directory.
- `ts`: Definition files for `TypeScript` will be generated. Useful if you use `TypeScript` in your project.

You need to pick the options from the list to match your project's needs. There is not much to choose from, but if you need to have your files both jQuery compatible and have `TypeScript` definition files, just use:

```
$ thrift --gen js:jquery,ts myfirst.thrift
```

Watch out, because you won't get any error message if you misspell the parameter; it will just be ignored. It's hard to debug such a situation, so just check your parameters twice.

Examining the code

The code that you generated will be in the `gen-js` directory. Inside the directory, there will be at least two files prefixed with your namespace.

One of them is suffixed with `_types.js` and contains the variables and constant that you created (in our example, this file's name is `myfirst_types.js`). Note that there are complex structures to handle the variables. Constants, on the other hand, are handled simply as JavaScript variables, for example:

```
myfirst.PI = 3.14159;
```

The other file bears the service's name (in our example, `MyFirstService.js`) and contains the client's objects.

If you declared more than one service or namespaces, more files will be generated accordingly.

If you used the `ts` option during compilation, there are also the `TypeScript` definition files with names ending in `.d.ts`.

Transport, protocol, and servers

Due to the simplicity of the implementation of JavaScript code to be used in the web browsers, the developer will only use one of the transport and protocol objects: `Thrift.Transport` and `Thrift.Protocol`, respectively. You can examine the implementation in the `lib/js/src/thrift.js` file, where the whole code is stored.

For obvious reasons, there is no server implementation in the client-side JavaScript.

Implementing and running the client

JavaScript client for Apache Thrift-enabled services is run by the web browser. The common scenario is to have a web application that collects some information from or posts to the service, which is going to be implemented in any other language.

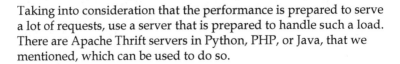

When developing services to be consumed by JavaScript from web applications that will be publicly available, please consider the security and performance of the setup.

From the security point of view, you should bear in mind that your whole service will be accessible for everyone, not only for those users who will use your web applications, but for anyone who would want to write their own client. Having this in mind, think about possible vulnerabilities: methods that modify the data or expose them in bulk. Consider exposing only those methods that won't do any harm if misused by somebody, and move other methods to the server side (that is, add an extra layer in PHP or Python). You shouldn't embed any authorization code (that is, usernames, passwords, API keys, and so on) in the JavaScript code, as it is easily readable by anyone.

Taking into consideration that the performance is prepared to serve a lot of requests, use a server that is prepared to handle such a load. There are Apache Thrift servers in Python, PHP, or Java, that we mentioned, which can be used to do so.

To construct the client for the Apache Thrift service in JavaScript, we will need the following components:

- The `thrift.js` library that can be obtained from the `lib/js/src/` directory in your Apache Thrift library
- The `gen-js` directory with files generated by the compiler
- An HTML page that contains the client code

As you already have the first two components, let's prepare the HTML document. For brevity, the layout is reduced to be as simple as possible; you are encouraged to work your way towards the expected result.

Let's have a look at the HTML code:

```
<!DOCTYPE html PUBLIC "-//W3C//DTD XHTML 1.0 Strict//EN" "http://www.
w3.org/TR/xhtml1/DTD/xhtml1-strict.dtd">
<html xmlns="http://www.w3.org/1999/xhtml" xml:lang="en" lang="en">
    <head>
        <meta http-equiv="Content-Type" content="text/html;
charset=utf-8" />
        <title>MyFirstService example</title>

        <!-- include the Apache Thrift library -->
        <script src="thrift.js" type="text/javascript"></script>

        <!-- include files generated by the Apache Thrift compiler -->
```

```
        <script src="gen-js/myfirst_types.js" type="text/
javascript"></script>
        <script src="gen-js/MyFirstService.js" type="text/
javascript"></script>

        <script type="text/javascript" src="http://code.jquery.com/
jquery-1.11.3.min.js"></script>

        <script type="text/javascript" charset="utf-8">
            // provide the service location - let's assume it's on
http://localhost:8080/MyFirstService
            var transport = new Thrift.Transport("http://
localhost:8080/MyFirstService");
            var protocol  = new Thrift.Protocol(transport);
            var client    = new MyFirstServiceClient(protocol);

            client.log("logfile.log");
            var mresult = client.multiply(6,7);
            $('#result').val(result);
        </script>

    </head>

    <body>
        <p>result of 6x7: <input type="text" id="result" value=""/></
p>
    </body>
</html>
```

As you see, this code is relatively simple in comparison to implementation in other languages.

If you want to use the variable types defined by you, that is, our MyStruct struct, it is very easy to instantiate them:

```
var ms = new MyStruct();
```

Then, work with it as with any other class to read or write values, for example:

```
ms.myi32 = 42;
$('#result').val(ms.myi32);
alert(ms.myi32);
```

To run the code, save it to the file, for example, MyFirstClient.html. Ensure that all the files that we listed before are accessible. Now, open your file in the web browser through a web server or directly. The client code will be run in the browser and the service will be called. The result will appear in the text field.

Ruby

Ruby is another very popular programming language used not only for web applications (that is, in the Ruby on Rails framework), but also for general scripting.

Generating the code

Apache Thrift's compiler has a limited number of special options for Ruby; there are only two. Run the following command to see them:

```
$ thrift --help
```

Look for the information about Ruby generators:

```
rb (Ruby):
    rubygems:          Add a "require 'rubygems'" line to the top of each
generated file.
    namespaced:        Generate files in idiomatic namespaced directories.
```

Let's explain both of them:

- `rubygems`: As the description states, it just adds the `require 'rubygems'` line on top of each file that is generated by the compiler.
- `namespaced`: The files that are generated are put in the directories with the names of the namespaces which you selected.

If you need both options, you can combine them:

```
$ thrift --gen rb:rubygems,namespaced myfirst.thrift
```

Watch out, because you won't get any error message if you misspell the parameter; it will just be ignored.

Examining the code

The code that you generated will be in the `gen-rb` directory. If you selected the `namespaced` option during the compilation, the files will be in the subdirectories of the names that are the same as your namespaces.

Inside the directory, there will be files with the names referring to your services with camel case changed to underscores, for example, our `MyFirstService` will be in the `my_first_service.rb` file.

Additionally, there will be a file suffixed with `_types.rb` with the data types we defined and the other one suffixed with `_constants.rb` with the constants. In our examples, these will be `myfirst_types.rb` and `myfirst_constants.rb`, respectively. The implementation of the data types is a little bit less complex than, for example, in Java or Python, and the constants are equally simple.

Let's have a look at the service files. In our example, the `my_first_service.rb` file contains the `Myfirst` module (being our selected namespace), and the `MyFirstService` submodule, containing `Client` and `Processor` classes followed with some helper structures. As you can see, the implementation is quite simple.

Transports

In addition to the most popular transports described in *Chapter 4, Understanding How Apache Thrift Works*, the Ruby implementation of Apache Thrift offers some other transports as well. You can look up the list in the code repository in the `lib/rb/lib/thrift/transport` directory.

Some of the nonstandard transports you may find particularly useful are:

- `IOStreamTransport`: This is a very simple transport wrapping two objects, one of which has the `read` method and the other, the `write` method (it provides them as arguments for the constructor).

- `MemoryBufferTransport`: This is another simple transport where the data is exchanged using the internal memory buffer

If you intend to use one of those transports, I suggest you examine the implementation to be sure how it works and if it fits your specific needs.

Protocols

The Ruby implementation of Apache Thrift offers all of the standard protocols mentioned in *Chapter 4, Understanding How Apache Thrift Works*. Additionally, it provides `MultiplexedProtocol`, which is not a standalone protocol but a decorator that you can use to deal with complex scenarios when you need to connect to multiple services running on one server (multiplexing).

Implementations of the protocols are in the `lib/rb/lib/thrift/protocol` directory, where you can examine them before using.

Servers

The Ruby implementation of Apache Thrift contains all of the popular servers that we mentioned in *Chapter 4, Understanding How Apache Thrift Works*. Moreover, it contains two more that you may find useful in certain scenarios. They are:

- `ThreadedServer`: This is a threaded server that spawns a new thread per each connection.
- `ThinHTTPServer`: This is an HTTP server, which makes use of Thin, which is a popular Ruby web server noted for its security, stability, and performance (see `http://code.macournoyer.com/thin/` for the details).

There is also `MongrelHTTPServer`, which you shouldn't use because it is deprecated; use `ThinHTTPServer` instead.

You can examine the implementations of the servers in the `lib/rb/lib/thrift/server` directory of the Apache Thrift package.

Implementing and running the service

In Ruby, everything is simpler; no interface to implement. It is enough to create a handler that contains all of the methods of the service that we want to expose. The methods should accept and return the variables of the declared types.

The following source code indicates how to do it. For brevity, the implementation details of the methods were omitted:

```ruby
# directory with code generated by Apache Thrift
$:.push('gen-rb')
# directory with the Apache Thrift library
$:.unshift 'thrift/lib/rb/lib'

require 'thrift'
require 'my_first_service'

class MyFirstHandler
    # empty constructor
    def initialize; end

    def log(filename)
      # implement log here
    end

    def multiply(number1, number2)
      # implement multiply here
```

```
      end

      def get_log_size(filename)
        # implement get_log_size here
      end

  end

  handler = MyFirstHandler.new()
  processor = MyFirstService::Processor.new(handler)
  transport = Thrift::ServerSocket.new(8080)
  transportFactory = Thrift::BufferedTransportFactory.new()
  server = Thrift::SimpleServer.new(processor, transport,
  transportFactory)

  server.serve()
```

To start the server, save this code to the `MyFirstServer.rb` file and run the following command:

$ ruby MyFirstServer.rb

Your server will be running on the localhost, port `8080`.

Implementing and running the client

To run the client using the Ruby Apache Thrift implementation, you need to prepare the network stack. Then, after connecting, you can call your remote procedures using the instance of your service's client that was generated by the compiler; in our case, it is `MyFirstService::Client`. Let's have a look at the example code, which is very simple and very similar to that of Python:

```
  # directory with code generated by Apache Thrift
  $:.push('gen-rb')
  # directory with the Apache Thrift library
  $:.unshift 'thrift/lib/rb/lib'

  require 'thrift'

  require 'my_first_service'

  transport = Thrift::BufferedTransport.new(Thrift::Socket.
  new('localhost', 8080))
  protocol = Thrift::BinaryProtocol.new(transport)
```

```
client = MyFirstService::Client.new(protocol)

transport.open()

client.log("logfile.log")
print client.multiply(14,3)

transport.close()
```

If you want to use variable types defined by you, that is, our `MyStruct` struct, it is very easy to instantiate them:

```
ms = MyStruct.new()
```

Then, work with it as with any other class to read or write values, for example:

```
ms.myi32 = 42
print ms.myi32
```

You can run your client by simply saving the code to the file, that is, `MyFirstClient.rb` and running the Ruby file from command line:

$ ruby MyFirstClient.rb

Of course, you can also embed the client code in your application, depending on your needs.

C++

C++ is one of the most popular programming languages these days. It is a universal, general purpose language, which is useful in a wide range of applications, including desktop, servers, networking, embedded systems, databases, and lots more. Apache Thrift is a natural companion for C++ to provide highly scalable systems characterized by high performance.

Generating the code

Apache Thrift's compiler offers a rich choice of options for C++. Run the following command to see them:

$ thrift --help

Look for the information about C++ generators:

```
cpp (C++)
    cob_style:       Generate "Continuation OBject"-style classes.
```

```
no_client_completion:
                 Omit calls to completion__() in CobClient class.
no_default_operators:
                 Omits generation of default operators ==, != and <
templates:       Generate templatized reader/writer methods.
pure_enums:      Generate pure enums instead of wrapper classes.
dense:           Generate type specifications for the dense protocol.
include_prefix:  Use full include paths in generated files.
```

The options are very specific and cater to the specialized needs of some projects.

You need to pick the options from the list to match your project's needs. It is possible to use more than one, for example, if you would like your code to have templatized reader/writer methods and use full include paths in generated files, use:

```
$ thrift --gen cpp:templates,include_prefix myfirst.thrift
```

Beware, you won't get any error message if you misspell the parameter; it will just be ignored. It's hard to debug such a situation, so just check your parameters twice.

Examining the code

The code that you have generated will be in the `gen-cpp` directory. In a convention similar to the Apache Thrift implementation in other languages, some of the files are prefixed with the namespace name (which is `myfirst` in our example), so the following files are generated in our example:

- `myfirst_constants.cpp`: This contains the definitions of the constants, which, similarly to other languages, is quite simple.

- `myfirst_types.cpp`: This contains the definitions of our custom data types along with the code to handle them.

- `MyFirstService.cpp`: This contains definitions of all the objects needed to handle our service along with `MyFirstServiceClient`, which is used to create the client.

- `MyFirstService_server.skeleton.cpp`: This is an extra file, which is very useful. It contains the skeleton of our service; we will use this file to implement our server.

All of the files (except the last one) are accompanied by header files (with the .h suffix).

Let's look at the `MyFirstService.h` file. It contains the `MyFirstServiceIf` interface that we will need to implement in order to have our service in C++:

```
class MyFirstServiceIf {
 public:
  virtual ~MyFirstServiceIf() {}
  virtual void log(const std::string& filename) = 0;
  virtual int multiply(const int number1, const int number2) = 0;
  virtual int get_log_size(const std::string& filename) = 0;
};
```

An interface is a description of the elements that the class which extends it has to have. Thus, you need to implement all of the methods of your interface for the service to exist; in this case, the `log`, `multiply`, and `get_log_size` methods you declared in your Apache Thrift document. The methods that you can override are marked with the `virtual` keyword.

The `MyFirstService.h` file also contains the `MyFirstServiceClient` class, which implements the `MyFirstServiceIf` interface and which you will use in your client application.

Transports

There is a wide array of transports available in the C++ implementation of Apache Thrift. You can look them up in the `lib/cpp/src/thrift/transport` directory. There are all of the most popular transports described in *Chapter 4, Understanding How Apache Thrift Works*.

There are also multiple nonstandard transports that you might find particularly useful:

- `TMemoryBuffer`: Transport reads from and writes to the memory buffer
- `THttpTransport`: Basic HTTP layered transport without any external dependencies
- `TPipe`: Transport that enables you to use Windows Pipes (a way of interprocess communication in Microsoft Windows)
- `TSSLSocket`: Sockets with added SSL security
- `TZlibTransport`: Transport with `zlib` compression

If you intend to use one of the transports, I suggest you examine the implementation to be sure how it works and if it fits your specific needs.

Protocols

In addition to the standard protocols that were discussed in *Chapter 4, Understanding How Apache Thrift Works*, the C++ implementation of Apache Thrift offers `TMultiplexedProtocol`, which is a decorator that helps you deal with multiplexing, that is, multiple services on one server.

Implementations of the protocols are in the `lib/cpp/src/thrift/protocol` directory where you can examine them before use.

Servers

The C++ implementation of Apache Thrift offers all of the basic servers mentioned in *Chapter 4, Understanding How Apache Thrift Works*.

You can examine the implementations of the servers in the `lib/cpp/src/thrift/ server` directory.

Implementing and running the service

Implementing the service is done by creating a handler class, which implements the interface that was generated by Apache Thrift; in our case, it is `MyFirstServiceIf`. Then, the server needs to be created.

As I mentioned earlier, the Apache Thrift compiler is kind enough to prepare the skeleton of the service for us — in our example, in the `MyFirstService_server. skeleton.cpp` file. It's a great convenience as the only job left for us is to implement the functions and tweak the server settings. Let's look at this file. For the sake of brevity, the implementation details of the methods are omitted:

```
#include "MyFirstService.h"
#include <thrift/protocol/TBinaryProtocol.h>
#include <thrift/server/TSimpleServer.h>
#include <thrift/transport/TServerSocket.h>
#include <thrift/transport/TBufferTransports.h>

using namespace ::apache::thrift;
using namespace ::apache::thrift::protocol;
using namespace ::apache::thrift::transport;
using namespace ::apache::thrift::server;

using boost::shared_ptr;

using namespace   ::myfirst;
```

```cpp
class MyFirstServiceHandler : virtual public MyFirstServiceIf {
 public:
  MyFirstServiceHandler() {
    // Your initialization goes here (if needed)
  }

  void log(const std::string& filename) {
    // implementation of log function goes here
  }

  int multiply(const int number1, const int number2) {
    // implementation of multiply function goes here
  }

  int get_log_size(const std::string& filename) {
    // implementation of get_log_size function goes here
  }

};

int main(int argc, char **argv) {
  int port = 8080;
  shared_ptr<MyFirstServiceHandler> handler(new
MyFirstServiceHandler());
  shared_ptr<TProcessor> processor(new MyFirstServiceProcessor(handl
er));
  shared_ptr<TServerTransport> serverTransport(new
TServerSocket(port));
  shared_ptr<TTransportFactory> transportFactory(new
TBufferedTransportFactory());
  shared_ptr<TProtocolFactory> protocolFactory(new
TBinaryProtocolFactory());
  TSimpleServer server(processor, serverTransport, transportFactory,
protocolFactory);
  server.serve();
  return 0;
}
```

Let's save this code to a new file, that is, `MyFirstServer.cpp`.

To compile and link your server code, run the following command:

```
$ g++ -DHAVE_INTTYPES_H -DHAVE_NETINET_IN_H -Wall -I/usr/local/include/
$ thrift --Igen-cpp *.cpp -L/usr/local/lib -lthrift -o MyFirstServer
```

Your server code will be in the `MyFirstServer` file. You can run it by using following command:

```
$ ./MyFirstServer
```

Implementing and running the client

Creating and running the C++ client code is straightforward, however the client code is not automatically generated by the Apache Thrift compiler. As with the implementation in other languages, you need to create the environment and then use the `MyFirstServiceClient` class.

Here's the code example:

```cpp
#include <iostream>

// MyFirstService header file
#include "gen-cpp/MyFirstService.h"

#include <transport/TSocket.h>
#include <transport/TBufferTransports.h>
#include <protocol/TBinaryProtocol.h>

using namespace apache::thrift;
using namespace apache::thrift::protocol;
using namespace apache::thrift::transport;

using namespace std;

using namespace myfirst;

int main(int argc, char **argv) {
    boost::shared_ptr<TSocket> socket(new TSocket("localhost", 8080));
    boost::shared_ptr<TTransport> transport(new
TBufferedTransport(socket));
    boost::shared_ptr<TProtocol> protocol(new
TBinaryProtocol(transport));

    MyFirstServiceClient client(protocol);

    transport->open();

    client.log("logfile.log");
    cout << client.multiply(6,7) << endl;
```

```
        transport->close();

        return 0;
    }
```

You can embed your client's code in your application, or just save it to the `MyFirstClient.cpp` file, compile, and link:

```
g++ -DHAVE_INTTYPES_H -DHAVE_NETINET_IN_H -Wall -I/usr/local/include/
thrift -Igen-cpp *.cpp -L/usr/local/lib -lthrift -o MyFirstClient
```

Your server code will be in the `MyFirstClient` file. You can run it by using the following command:

```
$ ./MyFirstClient
```

Summary

In this chapter, you learned about the implementation details of Apache Thrift for the most popular languages: PHP, Java, Python, JavaScript, Ruby, and C++. You are able to build servers and clients in those languages, and make use of different options that are offered for each of them.

In the next chapter, you will use these skills to dive deeper into the more advanced applications of Apache Thrift.

6
Handling Errors in Apache Thrift

You learned the basics of developing applications with Apache Thrift. Now it's time to tackle a more advanced, though important topic: handling application errors in general, and, more specifically, in the Apache Thrift environment.

It is highly unlikely that your application, service, or any other piece of software will be error-free. No matter how much time you spend debugging, testing, and fixing your software, some bugs will slip into the final product. If you look at most software products these days, they all have bugs, even those from major companies hiring thousands of developers and testers.

Errors may be caused not only by the malfunction of an application, but also due to wrong data, connection problems, or invalid operations. You develop services that consume data that's provided from the outside—external libraries or applications. This data may be invalid and your service may be unable to process it. Consider a simple example where the service is designed to work on integer values and gets random strings, or it is a service that performs mathematical divisions and you order it to divide by zero.

In this chapter, you will learn about the types of errors that you may encounter, and how to avoid or deal with them when they can't be dodged.

What are the type of errors that can occur?

To avoid errors or handle them, you need to understand what they are and what causes them. Errors in programming can be classified into three main categories:

- Syntax errors
- Runtime errors
- Logic errors

Most of the errors that you will need to handle are in the middle category (runtime errors); however, the other two categories are equally important.

Syntax errors

Syntax errors, also known as **compiler errors**, occur commonly when you mistype some part of a language or use it incorrectly. The most common causes of such errors are missing semicolons, brackets or parentheses, mistyped language statements, and so on.

They are easy to spot; code containing such errors won't compile (if the language is compiled, such as C++ or Java) or won't run (in the case of interpreted languages, such as PHP, Python, or Ruby). The compiler or interpreter will issue the error and terminate an execution as soon as it parses the file.

Runtime errors

Runtime errors occur when a program runs, which means that they weren't discovered by the compiler or interpreter. The code doesn't contain any mistakes or syntax errors; however, your application is required to do something. This may not be completed most of the time due to some restrictions or limitations of the environment, the nature of the supplied variables or because of errors in other parts of the system.

Some of the most common examples of runtime errors are as follows:

- **Division by zero**: This occurs when the variable supplied as a divisor (the value by which some other value is divided) is equal to 0; this may happen, for example, when a variable of some other type is casted to an integer or floating point number
- **Missing or inaccessible file**: This occurs when your application tries to open some file for the purpose of writing or reading, but it doesn't have proper permissions or the file is simply missing

- **Connection errors**: This occurs when your application tries to connect to some remote service, but it is inaccessible due to a network error (that is, the host is unreachable), missing or wrong login credentials, timeout, or any other cause that may prevent the connection from taking place.

Frequently, a programmer is not able to predict such errors. Sometimes, a network connection works, and at other times, it doesn't; users may supply the wrong kind of data, and misconfigurations can lead to files being inaccessible.

In most programming languages, the occurrence of such errors is communicated by throwing an exception. The key is to handle them so that the application can continue with its operations despite the error. In the upcoming sections, you will learn about the exceptions and how to handle them.

Logic errors

Logic errors are the hardest to find and fix because your code is successfully compiled or interpreted and it runs perfectly; no runtime errors are reported. However, logic errors cause your application to deliver results other than those that are expected. This may be due to the fact that you've used the wrong variable somewhere, read from the wrong file, or written to the wrong database. Sometimes, it is as trivial as using a plus sign instead of minus or wrong units.

In 1999, NASA's orbiter, worth $125 million, disintegrated in the Mars atmosphere, instead of staying in its orbit and performing scientific research and data collection. It was concluded that the cause of the error was that one piece of software supplied values in English units, while the rest of the system used the metric system.

Most frequently, such errors won't reveal themselves during compilation, the parsing process, or runtime. The errors will, however, impact the results of the program, which sometimes, as shown in the NASA example, may lead to a spectacular failure.

The best way to pursue and eliminate such errors is to cover your code with unit tests. Such tests examine the smallest testable piece of application—the units— to check whether they provide proper results. They should be run automatically after any major change.

The subject of unit tests is very broad and outside the scope of this book. Every programming language provides one or more libraries that are designed to make unit testing possible. There are also countless frameworks and software suites to make the testing process continuous and automatic. The method of preparing the tests first and then writing the code so that the tests pass is called **test-driven development** (TDD).

What are exceptions and how to handle them?

In our work, we will concentrate on runtime errors as these are the errors that may occur in your Apache Thrift-enabled application and you can (and should) handle them.

In most programming languages, exceptions work in a similar manner: when an error occurs at runtime, a special object is created. This object inherits from the basic exception or error class, depending on the language, and contains information on the nature of the problem. The execution of the program is interrupted and the exception object is passed to the runtime system (this is called **throwing an exception**), which, in turn, tries to handle it. Developers have the ability to define various exception handlers, which can catch the exception. These handlers specify the kind of errors they can handle — the type of exception objects that are accepted are listed in the handler's header. The inheritance path is taken into consideration here, so that handlers can be more or less general; they will accept all the exceptions of a given class and those deriving from it.

Let's have a look at this modified example from Python's manual, which illustrates the process of handling the exceptions, which we discussed earlier:

```python
import sys

class MyError(Exception):
    pass

try:
    f = open('myfile.txt')    // open myfile.txt file
    s = f.readline()          // read line from the file
    i = int(s.strip())        // cast read value to the integer
    if i == 42:
        raise MyError         // throw custom error if i = 42

// handle I/O errors
except IOError as e:
```

```
        print "I/O error({0}): {1}".format(e.errno, e.strerror)

    // handle variable type conversion errors
    except ValueError:
        print "Could not convert data to an integer."

    // handle my custom exception
    except MyError:
        print "The value was 42."

    // handle all other errors
    except:
        print "Unexpected error:", sys.exc_info()[0]
        raise
```

In this example, the code that we want to run is wrapped in the block beginning with the `try` statement. Our goal is to handle errors that might occur in this block; there are statements that read data from the file and cast a string variable to the integer, so we anticipate some of the errors that may occur; for example, when the file is missing or not readable (the `IOError` exception), or the string value can't be converted to the integer (the `ValueError` exception). As an illustration, I also added the custom `MyError` exception, which is thrown (using Python's `raise` statement; however, most languages use `throw` instead) when the value of the `i` variable is 42 (this doesn't make much sense, but illustrates that you can throw your own exceptions the same way as any built-in function).

In order to handle errors, there are several blocks of code beginning with the `except` statement (which is unique for Python, as in most programming languages, `catch` is the thrown exception being caught here instead) and the name of the exception class that's handled in this block. This is because every exception may be handled differently, and it is important to understand the nature of the possible error and the solution that we may offer. It is common to leave the last `catch-all` block, which will handle any unexpected exceptions left.

Handling exceptions in Apache Thrift

The errors that you have to care about most in your cross-language applications using Apache Thrift are runtime errors, over which you probably don't have much control. You may not be able to ensure that networks always work flawlessly and hosts are reachable, required files are accessible, and that all data is provided in the required format. Thus, you need to prepare for the worst-case scenario when none of them is working.

Every error has its own specific solution or measure that can be taken to handle it. You have to evaluate your situation and apply the relevant solution; for example, in some applications, when the host is unreachable, it is enough to try to connect to it repeatedly (this is common in mobile applications or when you try to connect to a well-known and relatively reliable third-party service, such as Google or Facebook), while in others, it is better to send a notification to the person responsible (for example, when your host is in the local network and you have administrative power over it).

Therefore, here we will discuss how to pass information about errors from a service to a client without getting into the details of how to handle specific errors.

An example code

In order to illustrate this, we will use slightly modified code from the previous chapters. For your convenience, you can download the code from Packt's website. We add one more method, named divide, that can easily give us some trouble; for example, when an attempt is made to divide by zero or the specified value is not an integer or float.

Here is the method declaration in `MyFirstService` in our Apache Thrift document:

```
double divide(1:double number1, 2:double number2) throws
(1:DivisionByZeroError zero_error, 2:WrongTypeError type_error)
```

We have two new exceptions, `DivisionByZeroError` and `WrongTypeError`, that we, of course, need to declare even though they are very simple:

```
exception DivisionByZeroError {
    1: string description
}

exception WrongTypeError {
    1: string description
}
```

In this chapter, we will be working with the Python service and PHP client; however, you can implement it in any other language supported by Apache Thrift.

I recommend that you copy the new `myfirst.thrift` file to a new directory along with the `thrift-0.9.2` directory containing the Apache Thrift libraries (the exact name may vary due to differences in version numbers).

After doing this, generate new Apache Thrift files:

```
$ thrift --gen py,php myfirst.thrift
```

Now, for convenience, copy the generated `MyFirstService-remote` file, which is useful for testing your service (we mentioned this in the previous chapter), to the current directory:

```
$ cp gen-py/myfirst/MyFirstService-remote .
```

To easily run it in our test environment, substitute the `import sys` directive at the top of the file with an indication of the proper paths (remember to substitute `0.9.2` with your version number):

```
import sys,glob
sys.path.insert(0, glob.glob('thrift-0.9.2/lib/py/build/lib.*')[0])
sys.path.append('gen-py')
```

To see the syntax of the `MyFirstService-remote` script, run it without any parameters. In the case of our tutorial example, the output will be like this:

```
$ ./MyFirstService-remote

Usage: ./MyFirstService-remote [-h host[:port]] [-u url] [-f[ramed]]
[-s[sl]] function [arg1 [arg2...]]

Functions:
  void log(string filename)
  int multiply(int number1, int number2)
  int get_log_size(string filename)
  double divide(double number1, double number2)
```

In our example, only the new `divide` method will be implemented — we will implement it in a moment so that we can play a little with our service.

Implementing the divide method

This time, we will actually implement the new method, something that I left to you earlier. We will do it step by step to see the outcome and think about the fixes that we need to apply.

Take the `MyFirstServer.py` file that you probably created while reading the previous chapter.

 If you didn't created the `MyFirstServer.py` file, you can download it from Packt's website. Note that the files in the archive that are supplied by the publisher have version names marked, that is, `MyFirstServer.v1.py`, `MyFirstServer.v2.py`, and so on, so you can easily examine the sequence that we follow here in the text.

Let's implement the basic version of the `divide` method of the `MyFirstHandler` class and save it:

```
class MyFirstHandler:
    def __init__(self):
        pass

// some methods here…

    def divide(self, number1, number2):
        return number1/number2
```

As you can see, the `divide` method does exactly what we want it to: it takes two arguments and divides the first by the other. Everything should work well. But, will it?

 As an extra task, I encourage you to implement other methods as well as think about error scenarios for them and implement exception handling.

Running the application without error handling

Let's run the server so that we can start testing it:

$ python MyFirstServer.py

When you run this command, you will see nothing, but your server should start listening to the specified port (which is `8080` by default) of your localhost.

Now we can run `MyFirstService-remote` to test various scenarios. The first scenario should be straightforward:

$ ./MyFirstService-remote -h localhost:8080 divide 84 2

42.0

We ordered our client script to contact the remote service and run the `divide` method with two parameters: 84 and 2. As you may have easily predicted, the result of dividing these two numbers is `42.0`.

 The .0 indicates that this is a floating point number. This is common notation in many languages; 42 is an integer and 42.0 is a floating point number.

So, nothing special here: our service works as expected. However, let's see what happens when we try to divide our number by 0—something that shouldn't be done:

```
$ ./MyFirstService-remote -h localhost:8080 divide 84 0
Traceback (most recent call last):
  File "./MyFirstService-remote", line 112, in <module>
    pp.pprint(client.divide(eval(args[0]),eval(args[1]),))
  File "gen-py/myfirst/MyFirstService.py", line 146, in divide
    return self.recv_divide()
  File "gen-py/myfirst/MyFirstService.py", line 159, in recv_divide
    (fname, mtype, rseqid) = iprot.readMessageBegin()
  File "thrift-0.9.2/lib/py/build/lib.macosx-10.10-x86_64-2.7/thrift/
protocol/TBinaryProtocol.py", line 126, in readMessageBegin
    sz = self.readI32()
  File "thrift-0.9.2/lib/py/build/lib.macosx-10.10-x86_64-2.7/thrift/
protocol/TBinaryProtocol.py", line 206, in readI32
    buff = self.trans.readAll(4)
  File "thrift-0.9.2/lib/py/build/lib.macosx-10.10-x86_64-2.7/thrift/
transport/TTransport.py", line 58, in readAll
    chunk = self.read(sz - have)
  File "thrift-0.9.2/lib/py/build/lib.macosx-10.10-x86_64-2.7/thrift/
transport/TTransport.py", line 159, in read
    self.__rbuf = StringIO(self.__trans.read(max(sz, self.__rbuf_size)))
  File "thrift-0.9.2/lib/py/build/lib.macosx-10.10-x86_64-2.7/thrift/
transport/TSocket.py", line 120, in read
    message='TSocket read 0 bytes')
thrift.transport.TTransport.TTransportException: TSocket read 0 bytes
```

Well, we know that something went wrong, but the message is rather cryptic. The description of the error, `TSocket read 0 bytes`, provides no idea about the nature of our mistake.

Let's think about what to do to handle such situations.

> One of the advantages of Apache Thrift is that it handles all the exceptions on the server side and passes them to the client so that you don't have to worry that an invalid operation will terminate your server process.

Adding error handling to the server

The work that we want to do here is simple: we need to recognize when an invalid operation is performed and throw (or as we call it in Python — raise) an exception, which will be then passed by the Apache Thrift interface to the client. This way, we are able to recognize that something wrong has occurred and can act accordingly.

The best way to see how some errors are handled is to write a small script or program in which we make such errors deliberately and see what exceptions are thrown. The resulting exceptions are ones that we would like to catch, process, and throw our own exceptions which are recognized by our client.

In Python, you may enter the interactive mode using the Python command, and then you can try some invalid operations (>>> indicates the prompt):

```
$ python
Python 2.7.8 (default, Oct 23 2014, 16:41:58)
[GCC 4.2.1 Compatible Apple LLVM 6.0 (clang-600.0.54)] on darwin
Type "help", "copyright", "credits" or "license" for more information.
>>> 84/2
42
>>> 84/0
Traceback (most recent call last):
  File "<stdin>", line 1, in <module>
ZeroDivisionError: integer division or modulo by zero
>>> 84/"two"
Traceback (most recent call last):
  File "<stdin>", line 1, in <module>
TypeError: unsupported operand type(s) for /: 'int' and 'str'
```

First, we divided 84 by 2 and it was successful. Next, we tried to divide 84 by 0 and we got the ZeroDivisionError exception. Then, we tried to divide 84 by a string (which, of course, couldn't be done, even if the string contained the word two) — the interpreter couldn't perform this operation, so it threw the TypeError exception (this means that we wanted to use a variable of an invalid type for this kind of operation).

With this exercise, we learned that we need to handle two exceptions: ZeroDivisionError and TypeError. In our situation, handling will mean passing our own exceptions to the client.

Let's do this in the `divide` method implementation in the `MyFirstService.py` file in the way that I described earlier:

```
def divide(self, number1, number2):
    try:
        return number1/number2
    except ZeroDivisionError:
        raise DivisionByZeroError(description="You tried to divide
%f by zero" % number1)
    except TypeError:
        raise WrongTypeError(description="You provided the
variable of wrong type.")
    except:
        raise MyError(error_code=1, error_description="Unknown
error.")
```

This way, we cover the most likely error, which is an attempt to divide some number by 0. Also, we cover a kind of situation where the wrong type will be provided (although implementation in many languages type casts anyway, and, as in PHP, will fallback the value to 0), and just in case we can handle virtually any error using the `catch-all except` statement without specifying the exception type.

Handling of the exceptions in this case means throwing our own exception with some customized description. This is, of course, a very simple example where we just pass one exception as another, but you can imagine a more complicated scenario where the error may be created in the algorithm created by you.

 Remember to restart your server after making any changes to its code; it won't reload automatically. To do so, if you run your server from the command line, press *Ctrl* + *C* in the window with the server and run it again.

Let's use our `MyFirstService-remote` script to perform an invalid operation:

```
$ ./MyFirstService-remote -h localhost:8080 divide 84.0 0
Traceback (most recent call last):
  File "./MyFirstService-remote", line 112, in <module>
    pp.pprint(client.divide(eval(args[0]),eval(args[1]),))
  File "gen-py/myfirst/MyFirstService.py", line 146, in divide
    return self.recv_divide()
  File "gen-py/myfirst/MyFirstService.py", line 171, in recv_divide
```

```
    raise result.zero_error
```

```
myfirst.ttypes.DivisionByZeroError: DivisionByZeroError(description='You
tried to divide 84.000000 by zero')
```

Still, the result is far from readable, but you can recognize something familiar: our own `DivisionByZeroError` exception. It was thrown by the server and received by our client. It wasn't caught properly— this is what we will do next.

Adding error handling to the client

Let's switch to our PHP client. You may find it in the `MyFirstClient.php` file that we prepared in the next chapter or just download it from Packt's website. Some minor changes are needed. As we are working with the socket server, substitute the `$server` variable accordingly:

```
$server = new TSocket('localhost', 8080);
```

You can also substitute all client calls (calls of methods of the `$client` object) with one call that will invoke the error that we need:

```
print $client->divide(84,0);
```

Let's run our script and see what happens:

```
$ php -f MyFirstClient.php
```

```
Fatal error: Uncaught exception 'myfirst\DivisionByZeroError' in /Users/
krzysztofr/work/chapter6/gen-php/myfirst/MyFirstService.php:844
```

```
Stack trace:
```

```
#0 /Users/krzysztofr/work/chapter6/gen-php/myfirst/MyFirstService.
php(228): myfirst\MyFirstService_divide_result->read(Object(Thrift\
Protocol\TBinaryProtocol))
```

```
#1 /Users/krzysztofr/work/chapter6/gen-php/myfirst/MyFirstService.
php(188): myfirst\MyFirstServiceClient->recv_divide()
```

```
#2 /Users/krzysztofr/work/chapter6/MyFirstClient.php(33): myfirst\
MyFirstServiceClient->divide(84, 0)
```

```
#3 {main}
```

```
  thrown in /Users/krzysztofr/work/chapter6/gen-php/myfirst/
MyFirstService.php on line 844
```

As you can see, our application received the exception, but it just wasn't able to handle it. Let's change our method call so that it is able to do this:

```
    try {
        print $client->divide(84,0);
```

```
    } catch (\myfirst\DivisionByZeroError $error) {
        print $error->description;
    } catch (\myfirst\WrongTypeError $error) {
        print $error->description
    } catch (\myfirst\MyError $error) {
        print $error->error_description;
    }
```

Note that the `$client->divide(84,0);` call was encapsulated in the `try` statement followed by the series of `catch` blocks.

Let's try running our script again and see what happens:

$ php -f MyFirstClient.php

You tried to divide 84.000000 by 0

As you can see, the stack trace could be substituted with any code you wanted when handling the exceptions; in this case, it was nice print with the original information gathered from the exception description.

This way our server and client gained the ability to handle the errors.

Advanced error handling

The example that we just looked at is quite simple with regard to catching an exception and passing it to the client. In more complex, real-life situations, errors will occur in the code that you write, so it will be the sole origin of the exception.

Error handling is not just printing the error description on the screen. Depending on the situation and the nature of the error, you may want to perform different actions to resolve the problem.

In some cases, it may be burdensome to create separate exception classes for every error that may occur. Some applications may provide very detailed information about the errors, causing dozens of separate exceptions to be distinguishable. In such cases, as in our `MyError` exception example, it is advisable to create one exception class with more detailed information about the error in a string variable and numeric error code in the integer variable (the latter is important for automatic error parsing):

```
    exception MyError {
        1: int error_code,
        2: string error_description
    }
```

You will be able to access MyError's variables in your code and act accordingly. Here's a PHP example of the `catch` statement:

```php
catch (\myfirst\MyError $error) {
    print "error code: " . $error->error_code . "; error description:
" . $error->error_description;
}
```

Summary

In this chapter, you learned about a very important part of application development—handling errors. This is especially important in services that work over networks and can be called from different clients. In such situations, errors are not uncommon.

Remember that handling errors is not optional, especially in real-life applications. This has to be done so that your applications work reliably and predictably.

In the next chapter, you will use all the knowledge that you've already gathered and work on example server and client applications from scratch. We will run several clients in different languages simultaneously to imitate real-life scenarios.

7
An Example Client-Server Application

Through this book, you have gathered a wide scope of knowledge about Apache Thrift, and how to use it with different programming languages. You learned about its internals, how to define your services, implement the client and server in different languages, and how to handle errors. You even ran your first simple services and clients.

Now we will put this information together to work on a bit more complicated application. The goal of this chapter is to provide a step-by-step tutorial to create clients and services with Apache Thrift, applying all the knowledge gained from the previous chapters.

This chapter has a deliberately planned structure, which resembles a typical workflow for such a project. I encourage you to use it as a template for your future work.

 You can write your code as you progress through this chapter or download it completely from Packt's website and just follow the changes.

Our example application

We will be working on a relatively simple application, but it will allow us to use all the skills we need. You can use this example idea, or you might want a little bit of a challenge and invent your own. This time, we will implement our methods in full so that the application is entirely functional.

We will use the following things that we learned throughout the book:

- Structs passed as arguments and the return values of functions
- Exceptions and how to handle them in the service and client
- Custom consts
- Enums
- Different types of functions: those that return some values and others that don't return any
- Including external IDL documents to our original Apache Thrift document
- Substituting type names using the `typedef` statement
- The service inheritance model

Our example will cover most of these elements and some others as well.

Planning out your work

As you now have a general idea of what we will be working on, let's plan our endeavor. This is not only necessary for this chapter to have a structure, but you may as well use it as a template for your work.

Planning is the most important part of every project—it is better to spend some extra time in the process of planning, rather than proceeding without a strategy and failing along the way. Due to this, we will spend some time planning before we actually implement our ideas.

The outline of our plan is as follows: first, we will formulate the general idea of our application. This means that we will describe what we want to achieve in normal human language and the tools we are going to use to do this. This may not only include a description of business needs, but also technical requirements or limitations. In real projects, this phase will be conducted with your client's representative, someone who's representing your users or business people. It is important to collect most of the vital requirements at this stage because all the work that follows depends on it. It is extremely difficult to get back to this phase when the project is halfway through.

Then, we will start to be a little bit more technical. We will think about representing the objects that we described previously with data structures available in Apache Thrift. In the next step, we will get a brief idea of what the methods in our service will look like, the arguments they'll take, the values that are returned, or whether there is a need for some exception handling (there will always be exceptions, isn't it?). All this will be documented in an informal way.

When we have our goals and a general idea of how to achieve them, it's time to start the actual development. The first of our development tasks is to prepare the Apache Thrift documents. We will plan their layout (remember that we want to have more than one in order to make use of the service inheritance) and then proceed with creating the files. We will compile these files using the `thrift` command for service stubs and other resources.

Next, we will implement the servers and clients for our service. This time, we will perform the full implementation of the server so that you are ready to test the solution and get some real results. After running the server and clients, we will test various scenarios—some correct and others erroneous. This will allow us to check whether the implementation is correct and the errors are handled properly.

In the last step, we will research what can be done next, and the possible improvements that can be made. In real-world projects, it is also a good habit to evaluate the success of the cumulative effort that's been put in.

This is the plan that we will be following in this chapter. After you complete it, you may call yourself experienced in the development of Apache Thrift services.

Let's begin!

Getting a general idea of the example application

Before we get into coding, we need to know what to expect and what we can do to fulfil our expectations.

It this case, our requirement is to have an application that will let us test various Apache Thrift capabilities and be easy to implement and test. We want to have the server in one language and clients in two other languages.

Let's name our service `MyToolbox` and expose three methods that will perform the following actions:

- The first method, `get_distance`, will return the distance, in kilometers (rounded up to the nearest integer), between two points on Earth, given their coordinates (we will use decimal degrees, whose format is popular in modern mapping applications, GPS devices, and so on, which express coordinates as decimal values instead of degrees, minutes, and seconds, and is used in cartography and navigation).

- The second method, `find_occurences`, will take a string and a regular expression and return a list of all the lines in the input string that match the regular expression.

- The third method, `save_to_log`, will take some strings and filenames and save the log entry to this file. We assume that if there is no such file, we will create it.

We want our service to handle most of the errors that we can foresee. We need to think about what errors may occur at this moment so that we can define the relevant error handling.

Let's prepare a list of possible errors:

Method	Possible errors
`get_distance`	• The coordinates are out of range, that is, the latitude is less than -90 degrees or more than 90 degrees, or the longitude is less than -180 degrees or more than 180 degrees • This presents the wrong format of input data (the arguments are not floating point numbers or cannot be converted to them)
`find_occurences`	• The regular expression that is given as a parameter is invalid (it's either syntactically invalid or the argument is of the wrong type) • The input text is to be matched is invalid
`save_to_log`	• The filename submitted is invalid, for example, in the filesystem, you are not allowed to create a file with this kind of a name; for security reasons, we won't allow any filenames containing characters other than letters, numbers, and dots • The system prevents us from creating the file, for example, our application has no right to write or create such a file • We arbitrarily require the message to be at least five characters long and will refuse to write shorter messages

Remember that in the planning phase, you may not predict all the error scenarios that may occur. Later on, during development, you may want to get back to this list and update it.

A technical overview of the application

As we now know what we want to achieve, this is the best time to plan the technical elements of Apache Thrift that we would want to use. This is still not the moment when we start coding; the effect of our work will be in pseudocode.

Pseudocode is an informal description of how a computer program or other algorithm works or will work. This code doesn't have to be parsable in any programming language and the syntax relies heavily on convention. The goal of pseudocode is to give the developer an idea of what should be coded in the intended programming language without going deep into the implementation details.

As the core of every service is its functions, we will start from them, and then draw the big picture.

get_distance

Let's start with the first function of our service, get_distance. This function will return an integer value, which will be the distance in kilometers between two given points. As the maximal circumference of Earth is just a little bit over 40,000 km, there is no possibility of having two points that are more than 20,000 km apart. Therefore, a 16-bit signed integer, i16, which can store values from -32,768 to 32,767, is more than enough to get a return value. It will be mapped to the best fitting integer in each language, for example, PHP has just one type of integer whose size is dependent on the platform. This is also the reason why we need to use signed integers, even though the return values will be equal to or greater than zero. For the sake of convenience, we can substitute the not-so-readable name of i16 with our own: distance. We will use typedef to do this:

```
typedef i16 distance
```

Now, let's think about how we will pass the coordinates to the get_distance function. We want to measure the distance between two points on Earth. Each point is represented by its coordinates, which comprise the latitude and longitude. These are called floating point numbers. Therefore, we can conclude that we need some structure that will hold this pair. As extra information, we may store the name of a particular point on Earth and its type (that is, a city, lake, or mountain). Let's write it down in the pseudocode:

```
struct Point {
    float latitude,
    float longitude,
    string name,
    point_type type enum [city, village, lake, mountain, landmark]
}
```

This is, of course, not valid Apache Thrift code, but it gives you some idea about what you will need. From the definition of the struct syntax, you know that you will need to define the `point_type` enum separately.

We previously defined two types of errors that we anticipate here are the coordinates that are out of range and also include the types of input arguments that are wrong. Without going into much detail, we may define two exceptions thrown by this function: `CoordsOutOfRange` and `WrongDataType`. I think that the latter exception may be used in the other functions too.

The last, but most important, thing that we need to define is how actually the function will work on the data it receives. This involves some serious math, but don't worry, we won't get into the details here. We will take some assumptions to simplify our work (that is, let's assume that the Earth is an ideal sphere and we don't care about rounding errors that much):

$$d = r \cos^{-1}\left(\sin\left(latitude_1\right)\sin\left(latitude_2\right)\right.$$
$$\left. + \cos\left(latitude_1\right)\cos\left(latitude_2\right)\cos\left(\left|longitude_1 - longitude_2\right|\right)\right)$$

In this formula, the following have been explained:

- *d*: This measures distance
- *r*: This is the radius of the Earth, which is approximately 6,371 km
- *(latitude1, longitude1)* and *(latitude2, longitude2)*: These are the coordinates of the first and second points on the Earth, respectively (they need to be converted to radians)

Whoa, looks overwhelming, right? Don't worry, it is easier than it looks, especially once I give you the exact code to use in your implementation.

 If you would like to read a little bit more about how to calculate distances on Earth, read these two informative Wikipedia articles at `https://en.wikipedia.org/wiki/Great-circle_distance` and `https://en.wikipedia.org/wiki/Geographical_distance`.

The algorithm for this method may look like this:

1. Take the coordinates of the points on Earth.
2. Check whether they are within the range of (-90,90) for the latitude and (-180,180) for the longitude. If not, throw an exception.

3. Convert the latitude and longitude to the radians (you need to multiply the value by $\frac{\pi}{180}$ or 0.017).

4. Substitute the values in the formula.

5. Round up the result to the nearest integer.

6. Return the result.

Now, we have all the pieces to put together in our method. Let's write its declaration in the pseudocode:

```
integer get_distance(Point point1, Point point2) throws
(CoordsOutOfRange, WrongDataType)
```

This is all we need for now.

find_occurences

The `find_occurences` method will take as the arguments some strings that may have one or more lines of text (separated by the new \n line separator) and the string containing the regular expression. Then, a list of the matches is returned.

Errors that we anticipate in this situation are not valid regular expressions in the argument, or the string to be matched against the regular expressions is not valid. The former may be `NoValidRegex` and the latter is `InvalidInputString`.

The algorithm that will be the core of our method is quite simple and needs no elaborate explanation. It is devised as follows:

1. Check whether the parameters are valid. If not, return an error.

2. Construct the regular expression object (depending on the programming language that will be used for server implementation) and parse the string.

3. Get the list of matches and return it.

Our function will return the list of strings as `list<string>`.

Let's have a look at the pseudocode of this method:

```
list<string> find_occurences(string string_to_match, string regex)
throws (NoValidRegex, InvalidInputString)
```

For now, this is everything we need to know about this method.

save_to_log

The `save_to_log` method is the last method and the simplest one. It gets the filename and a string with the message as the parameters. Then, it tries to save the received message to the given file. The constraints are that we want the message to be at least five characters long, and we want to take extra care not to do any harm to important system files, thus limiting the filename to letters, numbers, and dots. This way it is impossible to write to files outside the current directory (as, for example, it is impossible to use the / character).

This function won't have any return value (it will be `void`). We can't make it `oneway` (so the client won't wait for the result) because we need to handle the exceptions if they occur.

The exceptions that we want to throw from this function are as follows:

- `MessageTooShort`: This includes a message that has fewer than five characters
- `InvalidFileName`: This includes the filename that contains characters other than letters, numbers, or dots
- `CantWriteToFile`: This can be referred to if, for some reason, it is impossible to write to the file

The algorithm for this method can be devised as follows:

1. Check whether the message is of the required length. It should be five or more characters long; if it isn't, throw an exception.
2. Check whether the filename doesn't contain characters other than letters, numbers, and dots; if it does, throw an exception.
3. Open the file (create it if it doesn't exist), append the message to the end of the file, and close the file. If some error occurs, throw an exception.

Once we have this information, we can write the declaration of the function in the pseudocode:

```
void save_to_log(string message, string filename) throws
(MessageTooShort, InvalidFileName, CantWriteToFile)
```

This is everything we need to have for this method for now.

The server

We also need to think about the requirements toward the server. Let's say it is written in Python. It will use `TServerSocket` over `TBufferedTransport` and `TBinaryProtocol`. We will also use `TSimpleServer` as our project doesn't need high performance. By default, the server will run on port `8080`.

Clients

We will write two clients: one in PHP and the other in Ruby. Both of them will be run from the command line; however, you may modify them to your needs to be a part of a web application, more configurable command-line applications, and so on.

Now, we have defined the technical details of our methods, server, and clients. At this time, we have all the information we need to start developing our solution.

So, let's get to work!

Preparing the Apache Thrift document

Apache Thrift allows us to have a more complicated structure of the documents than a single file. It is especially useful if you want to have a set of basic tools to include in different services.

In our simple example, let's say we want to have a basic service, which allows logging messages to file. Any other service that we build has to have this capability. We also want some basic exceptions defined that are universal and can be used in any service, regardless of its specifics.

Therefore, we will split our definition into two Apache Thrift documents:

- `mybase.thrift` will contain basic universal components
- `mytoolbox.thrift` will contain our specific service

 You can type the files as we go or download them from Packt's website.

The basic toolbox – base.thrift

Let's identify the components that are universal, and we can use them not only in our `MyToolbox` service, but also in any other service in the future.

For sure, the `save_to_log` function is universal and we can use it in many different services. Thus, we will create `MyBaseService` that will include this function. As `save_to_log` uses three exceptions (`MessageTooShort`, `InvalidFileName`, and `CantWriteToFile`), they also have to be included in this file.

We may also consider the `WrongDataType` exception used by the `get_distance` function as quite universal as such an error may occur in many different functions.

Now it is a time to define these components one by one and put them in the `mybase.thrift` file. Let's start with the namespace. For convenience, it should be the same as the file and service names, and it should be kept constant through the programming languages:

```
namespace * mybase
```

All the components of this file will be available in this namespace (or module, depending on the language).

Now let's define the exceptions. Let's agree on a convention whereby they will have an attribute description, which will provide the description of the error. The definitions are rather simple:

```
exception MessageTooShort {
    1: string description
}

exception InvalidFileName {
    1: string description
}

exception CantWriteToFile  {
    1: string description
}

exception WrongDataType {
    1: string description
}
```

We may now define `MyBaseService` with just one function. This is based on the pseudocode that we prepared in the previous section, but of course it needs to comply with the Apache Thrift's IDL syntax:

```
service MyBaseService {

    void save_to_log(1:string message, 2:string filename) throws
(1:MessageTooShort err1, 2:InvalidFileName err2, 3:CantWriteToFile
err3)
}
```

Save everything to the `mybase.thrift` file. Just to be sure that the syntax is OK, try to compile it:

```
$ thrift --gen py mybase.thrift
```

If you got no output and the `gen-py` directory was created and populated with files, you're good to go!

The MyToolbox service – mytoolbox.thrift

This is the actual service that will make use of `MyBaseService`. What you need to start doing is including `base.thrift` in your new `mytoolbox.thrift` file:

```
include "mybase.thrift"
```

Now let's define the namespace for this service; the rules for the namespace are the same as the ones you saw previously:

```
namespace * mytoolbox
```

The next step is to define all the components that weren't already defined in our universal base document and are going to be used by the service.

Let's start with the return value for the `get_distance` function:

```
typedef i16 distance
```

We can make the Earth radius constant as this value is unlikely to change, but we want to have it defined in one place and use it through all the applications:

```
const i16 EARTH_RADIUS = 6371
```

We need to have the enum defining different types of geographical points:

```
enum PointType {
    CITY,
    VILLAGE,
    LAKE,
    MOUNTAIN,
    LANDMARK
}
```

Now, the `Point` struct will be passed as an argument to the `get_distance` function. Once again, we adapt the pseudocode prepared in the previous section for the IDL syntax:

```
struct Point {
    1:double latitude,
    2:double longitude,
    3:string name,
    4:PointType type
}
```

We need to have the declarations of all the exceptions. There are three of them left, and they are all are very simple; we also follow this convention set for the base exceptions:

```
exception CoordsOutOfRange {
    1: string description
}

exception NoValidRegex {
    1: string description
}

exception InvalidInputString {
    1: string description
}
```

Now we have everything that we need to declare the MyToolbox service and both of its functions. Have a look at the code and then we will examine it:

```
service MyToolbox extends mybase.MyBaseService {

    distance get_distance(1:Point point1, 2:Point point2) throws
(1:CoordsOutOfRange err1, 2:mybase.WrongDataType err2),

    list<string> find_occurences(1:string string_to_match, 2:string
regex) throws (1:NoValidRegex err1, 2:InvalidInputString err2)
}
```

As we want to incorporate the methods of MyBaseService into the MyToolbox service, we need the latter to extend the former. This is consistent with the object inheritance model, which is seen in most object-oriented programming languages. Similarly, you have to prefix any exceptions, constants, and so on, from the included file.

The declarations of the functions are based on the pseudocode, but are compliant with the IDL syntax.

Compiling the IDL files

That's it. Let's see if the syntax of the file is valid and compile the PHP, Ruby, and Python libraries:

```
$ thrift --gen py --gen rb --gen php -r mytoolbox.thrift
```

The -r option is needed when we want to include some files in our Apache Thrift document and want them to be parsed too. If you have got no output message and the gen-py, gen-php and gen-rb directories were created, you may be confident that the syntax of the file is correct. If you have got some error message, review the code and try to fix it (you can check out the downloadable source files for comparison).

Implementing the server

Our server will be implemented in the Python language. In this section, we will go through the script line by line, explaining each as we go along; you can type it in the file or download it from the repository.

So, let's open the MyToolboxServer.py file and go through its contents.

Imports

At the beginning, we need to import files that are necessary for the script to run:

```
import sys, glob
# path for file generated by Apache Thrift Compiler
sys.path.append('gen-py')
# add path where built Apache Thrift libraries are
sys.path.insert(0, glob.glob('thrift-0.9.2/lib/py/build/lib.*')[0])
```

These are the modules in the gen-py directory and the thrift-0.9.2 directory (the name depends on the exact Apache Thrift version you use).

> Remember to build the library by running the following commands:
> ```
> cd thrift-0.9.2/lib/py
> python setup.py build
> cd ../../..
> ```

Next, we need to import some of the modules and functions that will be used in the implemented service. The first line contains the re (regular expressions) module and its constants module; the second contains some mathematical functions used during calculations:

```
import re, sre_constants
from math import sin, cos, acos, ceil, radians
```

Then, we import the modules that are generated by Apache Thrift and are placed in the gen-py directory. We will use them through our implementation. We need to import both the mytoolbox and mybase modules, even though the latter is included in the mytoolbox.thrift file:

```
from mytoolbox import MyToolbox
from mytoolbox.ttypes import *
from mytoolbox.constants import *
from mybase.ttypes import *
from mybase.constants import *
```

What follows are the imports of the Apache Thrift libraries that we want to use—transports, protocols, and server. If you choose different ones, you need to, of course, import them instead:

```
from thrift.transport import TSocket
from thrift.transport import TTransport
from thrift.protocol import TBinaryProtocol
from thrift.server import TServer
```

Displaying errors on the console (logger)

Here is a tip that I didn't mention before. Normally, when some problems occur with your server script (that is, a syntax error or other exception that is not handled by your code), you won't get any useful hints about what went wrong. If you want to easily debug your script, you need to know what the problem was; to do this, you need to have a logger that will print errors on the console. To register the logger for TServer, use the following code:

```
import logging
logger = logging.getLogger('thrift.server.TServer')
logger.setLevel(logging.DEBUG)
ch = logging.StreamHandler()
ch.setLevel(logging.DEBUG)
logger.addHandler(ch)
```

This way, all the errors will be printed on the console where you can examine them and find solutions for them.

Implementing service methods

Now, we need to implement the service and its methods. The easiest way to do this would be to create a single handler class with all of the methods. However, it is better to use a convention that's similar to the one that we used in our Apache Thrift documents. We have a universal service, which is extended by the other more specific one. This way, we stay consistent through all the layers of the system, both in the service declaration in IDL and the server implementation.

To achieve this, we will create a similar architecture: we will extend `MyBaseHandler` (containing the `save_to_log` method) with `MyToolboxHandler` containing the `get_distance` and `find_occurences` methods.

Let's have a look at the implementation of the first handler class:

```
class MyBaseHandler(object):

    def __init__(self):
        pass

    def save_to_log(self, message, filename):
        if len(message) < 5:
            raise MessageTooShort(description="The message is too
short.")

        if re.search('/[^a-z1-9\.]/', filename, re.IGNORECASE) is not
None:
            raise InvalidFileName(description="The filename contains
forbidden characters.")

        try:
            with open(filename, 'a') as file:
                file.write(message + '\n')
        except IOError as error:
            raise CantWriteToFile(description="I/O error({0}): {1}".
format(error.errno, error.strerror))
        except:
            raise CantWriteToFile(description="Unknown error while
writing to file %s." % filename)
```

As you can see, this class has the __init__ empty constructor; however, you may add some code there if you need to. Then, we implement the `save_to_log` method, taking into consideration all the constraints that were defined previously, such as what arguments the method takes, what exceptions are raised, and when and what operations are being performed. If the documentation is good, the development boils down to putting all the pieces of the puzzle together using the right syntax.

Now we will do the same with `MyToolboxHandler`, which extends `MyBaseHandler`. Let's start by examining the first lines of the class implementation:

```
class MyToolboxHandler(MyBaseHandler):

    def __init__(self):
        pass
```

As seen earlier, this class has an empty constructor, but you can add some code here if you need to.

The implementation of the `get_distance` function in this class begins with four blocks validating the input parameters. First, we check whether both of the arguments are of the proper type. Then, we check whether the values of the coordinates are not outside of the required range. In case of any problem, the exception with proper information is thrown (or raised using Python's terminology).

As the code is a little convoluted here, the blocks are split into smaller chunks of code for better readability:

```
def get_distance(self, point1, point2):

    if not isinstance(point1, Point):
        raise WrongDataType(description="point1 is of wrong
type.")

    if not isinstance(point2, Point):
        raise WrongDataType(description="point2 is of wrong
type.")

    if \
            point1.latitude < -180 \
        or point1.latitude > 180  \
        or point1.longitude < -90 \
        or point1.longitude > 90:
            raise CoordsOutOfRange(description="Coordinates of
point1 are out of range.")

    if \
            point2.latitude < -180 \
        or point2.latitude > 180  \
        or point2.longitude < -90 \
        or point2.longitude > 90:
            raise CoordsOutOfRange(description="Coordinates of
point2 are out of range.")
```

```
        return \
            ceil(EARTH_RADIUS * \
            acos(
                sin(radians(point1.latitude)) * sin(radians(point2.
latitude))
                + cos(radians(point1.latitude)) * cos(radians(point2.
latitude))
                * cos(radians(abs(point1.longitude - point2.
longitude)))
                ))
```

The last statement in this function is the elaborate formula that I promised you earlier. Believe or not, the result will be the distance in kilometers between two points on the surface of the Earth. It is not perfect; the result may diverge from the real value by a significant fraction, but it is good enough for our needs. Note that we use the EARTH_RADIUS constant that was defined in the Apache Thrift file.

The next method is find_occurences, which returns a list of all matches against the regular expression in a given text. If there are none, an empty list is returned. Of course, the required validation is made and exceptions are thrown:

```
    def find_occurences(self, string_to_match, regex):

        try:
            return re.findall(regex, string_to_match)
        except sre_constants.error:
            raise NoValidRegex(description="Provided regular
expression '%s' is invalid." % regex)
        except TypeError:
            raise InvalidInputString(description="Cannot parse the
string to match.")
```

This concludes the implementation of our handler class.

Creating the server

The last part is known to you; it's the creation of the handler object and server, which can be started like this:

```
port = 8080

handler = MyToolboxHandler()
processor = MyToolbox.Processor(handler)
transport = TSocket.TServerSocket(port=port)
tfactory = TTransport.TBufferedTransportFactory()
pfactory = TBinaryProtocol.TBinaryProtocolFactory()
```

```
server = TServer.TSimpleServer(processor, transport, tfactory,
pfactory)

print "Starting server on port %d" % port
server.serve()
```

Running the server

That's it! The last thing that you need to do after saving the whole code to the
MyToolboxServer.py file is to run your server:

$ python MyToolboxServer.py

Now, your server will run and accept connections on port 8080.

Implementing and running clients

As the server is running, we now need to implement the clients. You should be
familiar with this part, so I will just remind you of the most important parts, leaving
something for you as homework.

Creating a client in PHP

When creating the client in PHP, we go through the standard procedure of including
the required files, registering namespaces, and creating the connection:

```php
#!/usr/bin/env php
<?php
define('THRIFT_PHP_LIB', __DIR__.'/thrift-0.9.2/lib/php/lib');
define('GEN_PHP_DIR', __DIR__.'/gen-php');

require_once THRIFT_PHP_LIB.'/Thrift/ClassLoader/ThriftClassLoader.
php';

use Thrift\ClassLoader\ThriftClassLoader;

$loader = new ThriftClassLoader();
$loader->registerNamespace('Thrift', THRIFT_PHP_LIB);
// register your namespace
$loader->registerDefinition('mytoolbox', GEN_PHP_DIR);
$loader->registerDefinition('mybase', GEN_PHP_DIR);
$loader->register();

// include here the protocols and transports that you need
```

```
use Thrift\Protocol\TBinaryProtocol;
use Thrift\Transport\TSocket;
use Thrift\Transport\THttpClient;
use Thrift\Transport\TBufferedTransport;
use Thrift\Exception\TException;

$server = new TSocket('localhost', 8080);

// create connection
$transport = new TBufferedTransport($server, 1024, 1024);
$protocol = new TBinaryProtocol($transport);
$client = new \mytoolbox\MyToolboxClient($protocol);

$transport->open();
```

Note that, as seen in the Python server, you need to register both the `mytoolbox` and `mybase` modules, even though the latter is included in the `mytoolbox.thrift` file.

Now is the time to play with the methods exposed by the service. Let's create two objects of the `Point` type:

```
$p1 = new \mytoolbox\Point;
$p2 = new \mytoolbox\Point;

$p1->name = "London";
$p1->type = \mytoolbox\PointType::CITY;
$p1->longitude = 51.507222;
$p1->latitude = -0.1275

$p2->name = "Kilimanjaro";
$p2->type = \mytoolbox\PointType::MOUNTAIN;
$p2->longitude = -3.075833;
$p2->latitude = 37.353333;
```

Note that you have to prefix the class or exception names with proper namespaces in this case; the `Point` class is in the `mytoolbox` namespace, so you should refer to it using the `\mytoolbox\Point` syntax, and do the same thing for the `PointType` enum.

Now, we will use the `$client` object to call the service. Wrap this call in the `try-catch` block as, on the second try, we will provide invalid data, which should cause our service to throw an error:

```
try {

    print "Distance p1-p2: " . $client->get_distance($p1, $p2) . "
km\n";
```

```
        // if one of the values is out of scope
        $p1->longitude = 200;

        print "Distance p1-p2: " . $client->get_distance($p1, $p2) . "
km\n";

    } catch (\mytoolbox\CoordsOutOfRange $e) {
        print "CoordsOutOfRange: " . $e->description . "\n";
    } catch (\mybase\WrongDataType $e) {
        print "WrongDataType: " . $e->description . "\n";
    }
```

As you will see during the test, on the second try, the exception would be raised and, of course, handled. The second message won't be printed.

Next, let's try the `find_occurences` method. We will submit the [a-z] regular expression, which will match every lowercase letter and use it against the randomly generated MD5 hash.

 The output of the MD5 message-digest algorithm is a 128-bit hash value, represented as a 32-digit hexadecimal number, which, in turn, is represented by a string of 32 characters consisting of digits from 0 to 9 and letters from a to f.

On the second attempt, we will submit an `[a-z]` invalid string, which is an incomplete regular expression. We expect that in such a situation, the `NoValidRegex` expression will be thrown:

```
    try {
        print "Looking for letters in random md5 string:\n";
        var_dump($client->find_occurences(md5(rand()), '[a-z]'));

        // this will fail
        print "Testing wrong regex\n";
        var_dump($client->find_occurences(md5(rand()), '[a-z'));

    } catch (\mytoolbox\InvalidInputString $e) {
        print "InvalidInputString: " . $e->description . "\n";
    } catch (\mytoolbox\NoValidRegex $e) {
        print "NoValidRegex: " . $e->description . "\n";
    }
```

We will see the result of this when we run the script.

The last step is to test the `save_to_log` function and try to break the rules by supplying a message that is too short:

```
try {
    date_default_timezone_set("UTC");
    $client->save_to_log("my test message " . date("Y-m-d H:i:s"),
"logfile.log");
    $client->save_to_log("shrt", "logfile.log");
} catch (\mybase\MessageTooShort $e) {
    print "MessageTooShort: " . $e->description . "\n";
} catch (\mybase\InvalidFileName $e) {
    print "InvalidFileName: " . $e->description . "\n";
} catch (\mybase\CantWriteToFile $e) {
    print "CantWriteToFile: " . $e->description . "\n";
}
```

As seen in the previous examples, the first attempt should be successful, while the second should fail.

Finally, remember to close the transport:

```
$transport->close();
```

That's it. Save the code in a file (for example, `MyToolboxClient.php`) and run it:

$ php -f MyToolboxClient.php

The result should be similar to this:

```
$ php -f MyToolboxClient.php
Distance p1-p2: 6968 km
CoordsOutOfRange: Coordinates of point1 are out of range.
Looking for letters in random md5 string:
array(13) {
  [0]=>
  string(1) "c"
  [1]=>
  string(1) "f"
  [2]=>
  string(1) "a"
  [3]=>
  string(1) "e"
  [4]=>
  string(1) "a"
  [5]=>
```

```
        string(1) "f"
        [6]=>
        string(1) "a"
        [7]=>
        string(1) "c"
        [8]=>
        string(1) "d"
        [9]=>
        string(1) "d"
        [10]=>
        string(1) "e"
        [11]=>
        string(1) "b"
        [12]=>
        string(1) "d"
}
Testing wrong regex
NoValidRegex: Provided regular expression '[a-z' is invalid.
MessageTooShort: The message is too short.
```

As expected, some of the remote function calls turned out to be successful, while others resulted in errors, but all of them were handled by wrapping the calls in the `try-catch` block. You can review the consecutive commands and printed results to examine the successful and unsuccessful calls.

Creating a client in Ruby

The second client will be written in Ruby. You may notice that, in general, this implementation is a lot briefer, but follows similar principles to the one in PHP:

```
# directory with code generated by Apache Thrift
$:.push('gen-rb')
# directory with the Apache Thrift library
$:.unshift 'thrift-0.9.2/lib/rb/lib'

require 'thrift'

require 'my_toolbox'

require 'digest/md5'

transport = Thrift::BufferedTransport.new(Thrift::Socket.
```

```
new('localhost', 8080))
protocol = Thrift::BinaryProtocol.new(transport)
client = Mytoolbox::MyToolbox::Client.new(protocol)

transport.open()

print client.find_occurences(Digest::MD5.hexdigest("hello world"),
'[a-z]')

transport.close()
```

As you are already familiar with how to call the service and test the functions, I will leave the details of the function calls to you. In this case, we call only one function, find_occurences, to parse the MD5 hash. You may add extra calls to test different scenarios, and use the try-catch blocks to handle the errors.

Before you run the script, note that in the 0.9.2 version of Apache Thrift, there is a bug when you try to include other IDL documents, which prevents the scripts from running. You need to edit the file by hand; in our case, this means that you need to remove the extra reference to the module name in line 8 of the mytoolbox_types.rb file.

Instead of require 'mybase/mybase_types', it should be require 'mybase_types'.

Note that this bug may or may not occur in different versions of Apache Thrift.

To run your script, just type the following command:

$ ruby MyToolboxClient.rb

The result should be similar to this:

$ ruby MyToolboxClient.rb
["b", "a", "f", "f", "d", "b", "a", "b", "d", "c", "d", "c", "f"]

Further testing and other exercises

In our examples, we tried to submit some valid and invalid data to see how the service performs and if we are able to handle the errors properly. We didn't, however, test every possible scenario.

As an extra exercise, I suggest that you attempt the following tasks:

- Testing each of the functions in the Ruby client with both valid and invalid arguments

- Testing border cases and different combinations of valid and invalid parameters

- Writing automatic unit tests for the methods implemented in the server

- Experimenting with different transports, protocols, and servers

- Adding client and server code as a module to bigger applications, for example, written in some framework

- Running performance tests and comparing response times under different conditions

I hope that this (incomplete) list of possible solutions will inspire you to expand your Apache Thrift experience further beyond the basics covered in this book.

Summary

In this chapter, we covered everything that you learned up to this point in one service and three different applications. You were able to use all the language's capabilities to create your Apache Thrift service.

You not only recalled the technical details, but also got to know the optimal process that leads to creating the service and clients. Remember this method in future so that you can plan and implement your applications in an organized and structured manner. This way of working will let you meet requirements in an easier manner and with less effort, with the whole process being transparent and comprehensible.

In the final chapter, we will wrap things up with some examples of advanced usage of Apache Thrift. You will get some tips on using it in production environments and learn about how it is leveraged by the top companies.

8
Advanced Usage of Apache Thrift

If you have made your way all the way to this chapter, you have enough knowledge to design and develop your own services using Apache Thrift on a variety of platforms. In this chapter, I will provide you with extra information that you may use to expand your skills to work on complex projects solving real problems. You will also see that Apache Thrift is a powerful tool used by well-known companies, such as Facebook, Twitter, or Evernote, to power their core products.

I will mention several different topics that, I hope, you will treat as a starting point and inspiration in your journey to advance your Apache Thrift skills. The goal of this chapter is to provide as many pointers to useful directions as possible.

Apache Thrift in production

Through this book, you learned a lot about how to use Apache Thrift to suit your needs. However, as I mentioned a few times on various occasions, when working in a production environment, you must take into consideration lots of issues that are not that important in the development environment, such as performance, security, version control, and many more.

Let's go through some of the most important topics. I will cover them in enough detail to allow you to do further research and then introduce them in your project. Some of them are tightly related to Apache Thrift, while others are generic, but they will undoubtedly be useful and necessary.

Code version control systems

This topic will be mentioned briefly as it is not strictly Apache Thrift-related; however, it's of very high importance in every programming project, no matter what language is used.

Various code **version control systems (VCSs)** are popular right now, with Git (`https://git-scm.com/`) and Mercurial (`https://www.mercurial-scm.org/`) being the leaders in the open source community.

I hope that you are currently using one of them, but if not, let me convince you to do so by briefly mentioning the most important advantages of VCSs:

- **Security (backup)**: Your code not only stays on your computer, but you may also push it to a remote repository, sparing yourself trouble in case something bad happens to your hard drive.

- **Collaboration**: You may work independently on the same code base with other developers. It is even possible to work on the exactly the same file; the version control system will take care of merging the changes for you (of course, when the differences are more complicated, it may need to ask you for help).

- **Version control**: The most important feature of VCSs is that if you wish, you may restore your whole code base or just one file to any time in the past in order to recover some content, track bugs, or run the previous version of your software. You are able to work simultaneously on many versions of the software by utilizing the branching model and precisely tracking the changes.

- **Code delivery**: A centralized code repository may be also used as a tool to deliver the code to many machines instead of copying files to every server from the central one; just order each of the servers to pull the code from the repository. Most automated build systems integrate with Git or Mercurial by default.

You may include Apache Thrift files in your project's code repository or create a separate repository, depending on your needs and the size of the project.

Code deployment

When your system runs on more than one server, proper deployment starts to be a challenge. Very often, you need to run the same command on many machines simultaneously or according to some specific plan—it is impossible to log in and do this manually. In such situations, you should consider using automation software that will run all the deployment scripts and commands for you. Such software allows you to define what commands should be run on which machine.

Let's consider the simplest example from Fabric's (http://www.fabfile.org/) documentation, slightly modified by me, to illustrate the advantages of such software:

```
from fabric.api import run

def host_type():
    run('uname -s')
```

Running this Python script with hostnames as the parameters will yield this:

```
$ fab -P -H localhost,host1,host2 host_type
[localhost] run: uname -s
[localhost] out: Darwin
[host1] run: uname -s
[host1] out: Linux
[host2] run: uname -s
[host2] out: Linux


Done.
Disconnecting from localhost... done.
Disconnecting from host1... done.
Disconnecting from host2... done.
```

As you can see, the command was run on different machines simultaneously. This is an extremely simple example, but you can easily imagine how it may be expanded to run some deployment commands for a complex system. In a simple scenario, you may want each machine to pull the code from the repository, run some deployment scripts, and restart the services. Using this or a similar tool, you may do it at once without logging in to all of the servers.

Besides Fabric, there are other similar tools, some of them more complicated, offering a wide variety of options:

- **Ansible** (https://github.com/ansible/ansible)
- **Capistrano** (http://capistranorb.com/)
- **Chef** (https://github.com/chef/chef)
- **Puppet** (https://github.com/puppetlabs/puppet)

I suggest that you try using them in your project if you have two or more machines on which you need to deploy your code.

Apache Thrift versioning

Versioning in the context of services is a little bit different from code version control. Here, the issue that needs to be taken care of is the backward compatibility of your service with regard to different client versions (especially older ones).

In a perfect situation, both the server and clients run the same version of the software. However, this is rarely possible in the real world. An extreme example of this is a situation where the client software using our service is installed on millions of users' computers — it is hard to get them all to update at the same time, and we can't render the service unusable for old versions of the software.

However, even in systems that are completely under our control, when the services and clients are communicating internally, it is often impossible or not desirable to update all of the software at once. Many companies (for example, Facebook) deploy some of their updates to a part of their servers to check whether they're working properly and follow with the rest when they see that everything is OK.

Apache Thrift has built-in features that support versioning with regard to service arguments. You may recall the `get_distance` function from the previous chapters. Let's call it **version 1**:

```
distance get_distance(1:Point point1, 2:Point point2)
```

Both arguments have their numbers. If, let's say, we want to add an argument in the future, it is easy to do so:

```
distance get_distance(1:Point point1, 2:Point point2, 3:Point point3)
```

Let's call this **version 2**.

When Apache Thrift service's function gets an argument that it doesn't recognize, it is ignored. On the other hand, when there is an extra argument but its value isn't passed to the function, it gets the default value. This way, version 1 clients are still able to communicate with version 2 services even if you add and remove parameters. This special case occurs when you add the `required` keyword to the argument. Then, it is required for every call and if the client doesn't supply it, Apache Thrift will issue an error.

Remember that when you manipulate with arguments of functions, not to use the same identifier for different arguments. If you need to remove some argument and add another, just use a different ID; take a look at this example:

```
distance get_distance(1:Point point1, 3:Point point3, 4:string
description)
```

Note how we removed the second argument, 2:Point point2, but added the fourth 4:string description. There is an argument of ID 2 missing, but this is perfectly correct.

Another trick that makes passing different arguments easier is to pass just one struct as the argument for the method. This struct is a container for different sets of arguments. The function declaration always will look like this:

```
distance get_distance(1:Parameters params)
```

However, the Parameters struct may be different depending on the version. For example, in version 1, it would be:

```
struct Parameters {
    1:Point point1,
    2:Point point2
}
```

In version 2, it would be:

```
struct Parameters {
    1:Point point1,
    2:Point point2,
    3:Point point3
}
```

And finally in version 3, it would be:

```
struct Parameters {
    1:Point point1,
    3:Point point3,
    4:string description
}
```

As with methods, the same rule applies here: if you declare some variable as required, it has to stay this way till the end or you will risk that your service won't be backward compatible (which means that older clients will not work with it).

The versioning principle of structs applies, of course, to not only those structs that are containers for method parameters, but also to every struct used in the Apache Thrift document in general.

Apache Thrift performance

On Apache Thrift's website, there is a list of values that developers aim to embody when designing and developing this framework. One of the values is:

> *"Performance. Strive for performance first, elegance second."*

This is really a good description of the framework: as you probably went through its documentation and maybe looked at some code, you know that in many places it is far from being elegant. On the other hand, it keeps its promise of performance by providing a wide array of possible choices for developers who want to scale their application to achieve better results.

As requests are handled by the server, this is the main point where performance is impacted. We discussed what servers are available in each language in *Chapter 4, Understanding How Apache Thrift Works*, and *Chapter 5, Generating and Running Code in Different Languages*.

`TSimpleServer`, which is present in Apache Thrift libraries for most programming languages, is, as the name suggests, the simplest library and the easiest to configure, but its capabilities are limited to development environments or some small and not very demanding solutions, as it is capable of serving only one client at a time.

When researching what server to choose in your case, I recommend that you follow this approach:

1. Check what servers are available in the Apache Thrift library for your programming language.

2. Then, review the description of the selected servers in this book and also in the source files of the servers in the Apache Thrift code repository.

   Unfortunately, there is no official written documentation for most of them

3. As the final step, you should run your own performance benchmark, taking into the consideration the specifics of your project.

The authors of MapKeeper—the Apache Thrift-based key-value store with various storage backend (available as an open source application on GitHub at `https://github.com/m1ch1/mapkeeper`)—conducted research on the performance of Java and C++ servers available in Apache Thrift libraries using MapKeeper's benchmark tool, which you can also use by yourself. I will briefly discuss their findings.

Comparing Java servers

The authors of the *Thrift Java Servers Compared* document (`https://github.com/m1ch1/mapkeeper/wiki/Thrift-Java-Servers-Compared`) compared various Java servers available in the Apache Thrift library. They conducted tests on the following pairs:

- `TNonblockingServer` versus `THsHaServer`
- `THsHaServer` versus `TThreadedSelectorServer`
- `TThreadedSelectorServer` versus `TThreadPoolServer`

These authors compared the throughput (number of requests per second) and latency (response time) in relation to the number of consecutive clients. The results range from 10 reqs/s and a 1000 ms latency for `TNonblockingServer` to around 275,000 reqs/s for TThreadPoolServer and 5-45 ms latency for `TThreadedSelectorServer`.

The general conclusion of the research is that `TThreadedSelectorServer` would be the best solution in most cases. `TThreadPoolServer` offers better throughput but at the expense of running many concurrent threads.

Comparing C++ servers

Another good research document resulting from the MapKeeper authors' work is the comparison of servers available in the Apache Thrift library for the C++ language (`https://github.com/m1ch1/mapkeeper/wiki/TThreadedServer-vs.-TNonblockingServer`). They compared `TThreadedServer` and `TNonblockingServer`, once again comparing the throughput and latency. `TThreadedServer` obviously won in both categories with 300,000 reqs/s and a latency of less than 1 ms. `TNonblockingServer` was less performant with fewer than 50,000 reqs/s and a latency of over 7 ms.

In conclusion, the former is recommended, unless you plan to serve more than 10,000 clients concurrently (the so-called C10K problem), when the latter might be a better choice.

If you are not satisfied with the default options provided by Apache Thrift, consider scaling your system by adding an extra layer on top, such as the load balancer, which will distribute the load evenly among many similar services. You should also check out extra solutions developed by companies using Apache Thrift in high-performance environments. With the need for more performant services, these companies worked on better solutions, some of them now available as open source. You will read more on this in the second half of this chapter.

Service multiplexing

As you learned in the previous chapters, Apache Thrift servers are run on a specified port on which they listen and wait for incoming connections. This is convenient when you want to expose one service. However, what about a situation where you would like to provide access to 2, 3, 10, or 50 services? Imagine the trouble of running theses services as 50 separate servers on 50 separate ports. How much administration work would be needed, and how hard it would be to ensure the security of all the services.

This problem is not an imaginary one—it is not uncommon for an enterprise to have the need to expose more than a one or two services. Fortunately, there is a solution for this, which I briefly mentioned earlier: multiplexing.

Multiplexing is the ability to expose multiple services through one server and on one port. Not much work is really required here; you just need to use a proper multiplexed protocol. This concept is illustrated in the following figure:

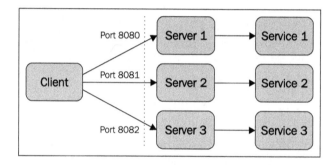

This is the basic way to expose the services. Every server runs separately and listens on a different port (8080, 8081, and 8082 are used in this example). A client needs to be configured and connected to multiple different endpoints. When these endpoints change (for example, when the hostname or port number is changed), all of the configurations need to be updated. This leads to maintainability issues.

Now, how does the structure look when we use multiplexing?

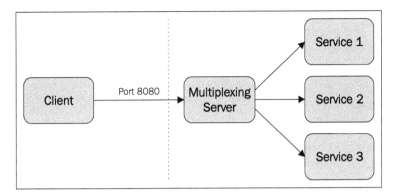

When we multiplex the services, only one server is exposed on a single port. It is the server's job to route the requests to proper services. Clients need to have only one endpoint in their configuration (the hostname and port number) so that maintenance is easier. The same goes for the server's administrators who have only one instance to deal with.

Let's look at the examples. In Java, you need to use `TMultiplexedProcessor` in the server and register the services' processors:

 You can download the following code from Packt's website.

```
import org.apache.thrift.server.TServer;
import org.apache.thrift.server.TServer.Args;
import org.apache.thrift.server.TThreadPoolServer;
import org.apache.thrift.transport.TServerSocket;
import org.apache.thrift.transport.TServerTransport;
import org.apache.thrift.TMultiplexedProcessor;

// import code generated by Apache Thrift compiler
import myservices.*;
```

```
public class MyMultiplexedServer {

    // define separate handlers and processors for both services
    public static Service1Handler handler1;
    public static Service1.Processor processor1;

    public static Service2Handler handler2;
    public static Service2.Processor processor2;

    public static void main(String [] args) {
        handler1 = new Service1Handler();
        processor1 = new Service1.Processor(handler1);

        handler2 = new Service2Handler();
        processor2 = new Service2.Processor(handler2);

        TMultiplexedProcessor mprocessor = new
TMultiplexedProcessor();

        // register processors for both services with multiplexed
processor
        // note the labels for both services
        mprocessor.registerProcessor("Service1", processor1);
        mprocessor.registerProcessor("Service2", processor2);

        // the rest is similar as for the single service
        Runnable server = new Runnable() {
            public void run() {
                myserver(mprocessor);
            }
        };

        new Thread(server).start();
    }

    public static void myserver(TMultiplexedProcessor processor) {
        TServerTransport serverTransport = new TServerSocket(8080);
        TServer server = new TThreadPoolServer(new TThreadPoolServer.
Args(serverTransport).processor(processor));
        System.out.println("Starting multiplexed server on port
8080...");
        server.serve();
    }

}
```

As you must have noticed, here, we used the code from *Chapter 5, Generating and Running Code in Different Languages,* so you can compare it with the multiplexed version. We use `Service1` and `Service2` for instructional purposes. We need to create separate handlers and processors for them. Let's look at excerpts from the preceding code:

```
public static Service1Handler handler1;
public static Service1.Processor processor1;

public static Service2Handler handler2;
public static Service2.Processor processor2;
```

and:

```
handler1 = new Service1Handler();
processor1 = new Service1.Processor(handler1);

handler2 = new Service2Handler();
processor2 = new Service2.Processor(handler2);
```

Then, these processors need to be registered with `TMultiplexedProcessor`:

```
TMultiplexedProcessor mprocessor = new
TMultiplexedProcessor();

// register processors for both services with multiplexed
processor
// note the labels for both services
mprocessor.registerProcessor("Service1", processor1);
mprocessor.registerProcessor("Service2", processor2);
```

Note that we using the services' names as labels that will distinguish them when the clients send their requests.

The rest is similar to the regular server code for the single instance: the server is started and it occupies only one designated port. The processor will be able to route the requests to the called services.

Now let's take a look at how multiplexing is reflected on the client's side:

```
// Import code generated by Apache Thrift compiler
import myservices.*;

import org.apache.thrift.transport.TTransport;
import org.apache.thrift.transport.TSocket;
import org.apache.thrift.protocol.TBinaryProtocol;
import org.apache.thrift.protocol.TProtocol;
import org.apache.thrift.protocol.TMultiplexedProtocol;
```

```
public class MyMultiplexedClient {
    public static void main(String [] args) {

        TTransport transport = new TSocket("localhost", 8080);
        transport.open();

        TProtocol protocol = new  TBinaryProtocol(transport);

        // create protocol and clients for both services
        // remember about the labels - the same as in the server
        MultiplexedProtocol protocol1 = new
TMultiplexedProtocol(protocol, "Service1");
        Service1.Client client1 = new Service1.Client(protocol1);

        MultiplexedProtocol protocol2 = new
TMultiplexedProtocol(protocol, "Service2");
        Service2.Client client2 = new Service2.Client(protocol2);

        // call remote functions using the client objects
        client1.somefunction(42);
        client2.otherfunction("abc");

        transport.close();
    }
}
```

We need to make the client aware of multiplexing. We do this by wrapping the regular protocol with TMultiplexedProtocol. That's it; we can call functions from both the services. Note that we need to use the same labels as the ones used in the server.

As you can see, multiplexing in Apache Thrift is relatively simple, but it is a powerful tool when you need to serve many services at once. There are more complex solutions when you need them, for example, to include not only Thrift, but also other services in your multiplexing. You will find more on this in the latter part of this chapter.

Security issues

Security is an important issue when dealing with services that are exposed to clients. It doesn't matter if a local service is available only to clients in the local network, or if it is a public API used by millions; security is always something that shouldn't be ignored. Even when designing internal services, you shouldn't assume that the environment is secure by definition. Other machines in the network may be compromised or behave erratically.

General security tips

There are some general security tips that apply to every service, regardless of whether it is based on Apache Thrift or some other technology or framework. You should remember them even if you develop a simple website.

The two most important elements are **authentication** and **authorization**. Though they are often confused with each another, they don't mean the same thing. Authentication is the process whereby the identity of a connecting client (be it a person, a service, an application, and so on) is confirmed. In the simplest and most common scenario, it is a pair of usernames and passwords. These parameters are checked against records in the database and, if they match, the client is considered authenticated. Quite often, services use the API key instead of the username/password pair. Such a key is a long, alphanumeric string (for example, the Amazon Web Service API key may look like `wJalrXUtnFEMI/K7MDENG/bPxRfiCYEXAMPLEKEY`). This solution is considered to be more secure as these keys are generally longer than a regular password; therefore, they are harder to break, may be freely assigned and revoked (it is possible to have multiple keys per account), or can even have different permissions in the scope of a single user account. Due to this, you may consider using API keys instead of the username/password pair when authenticating clients.

Authorization is a process of defining an access policy. So, when we have an already authenticated client (this means that we know its identity), we need to assess what the client is permitted to do. As with any other system, not everyone is allowed to perform any action. Based on internal records, you should grant the client access to only those actions that are allowed to be performed.

Especially when exposing services externally, you should carefully plan which actions should be available for anonymous users. This is strongly dependent on business needs, but as a rule, this practice should be avoided, for example, exposing large sets of data in bulk for download. Let's imagine that you have a classified ad service; you don't want someone to download your whole ad set and publish it on their website, right?

Data privacy is another important security rule for any application in general, but especially the service. This means that users should have access only to data that they are supposed to see. For example, a customer should have access only to his transactions; he shouldn't be able to view other peoples' transactions, for example, by substituting the transaction identifier variable.

Transport Layer Security/Secure Sockets Layer

We earlier discussed securing the service when the client has access to it, but what about the connection itself? In many environments, communication between the client and the server may be eavesdropped on by an attacker. To provide privacy to the transmission, we need to use the **Transport Layer Security** (TLS) protocol (frequently referred to as **SSL** or **TLS/SSL**). This protocol is commonly used to secure web applications, e-mail communication, messaging, and so on. You may know it from your experience, for example, when visiting websites whose address begins with `https://`.

Without going into much detail, security when using TLS is derived from the fact that the transmission is encrypted.

We will be working on the Java example code that we have already used in the previous section on multiplexing.

 You can download the code from Packt's website. The files are named `MySecureMultiplexedServer.java` and `MySecureMultiplexedClient.java`.

Generating keystores

To have communication encrypted, we need to have a keystore on the server (containing the public and private keys and the certificate) and a truststore with the certificate and the public key on the client.

We will use the keytool (shipped with Java) to create both of these files. Our certificates will be self-signed.

First, let's create a keystore. To do this, use the following command. You will be asked to enter a new password for the keystore and to provide some information about the unit issuing the key. This information is included in the certificate, so it should be valid. At the end, you need to type `yes` to confirm the validity of the information:

```
$ keytool -genkeypair -alias mykey -keyalg RSA -validity 365
Enter keystore password:
Re-enter new password:
What is your first and last name?
  [Unknown]:  John Smith
What is the name of your organizational unit?
  [Unknown]:  IT Department
What is the name of your organization?
```

```
[Unknown]:  ACME Corporation
What is the name of your City or Locality?
   [Unknown]:  Warsaw
What is the name of your State or Province?
   [Unknown]:  mazowieckie
What is the two-letter country code for this unit?
   [Unknown]:  PL
Is CN=John Smith, OU=IT Department, O=ACME Corporation, L=Warsaw,
ST=mazowieckie, C=PL correct?
   [no]:  yes


Enter key password for <mykey>
   (RETURN if same as keystore password):
```

The parameters of the `keytool -genkeypair` command are:

- `-alias mykey`: This is the name of the keystore; it can be anything you wish

- `-keyalg RSA`: This is the key that will be generated using the RSA algorithm

- `-validity 365`: This key will be valid for 365 days (after this, you need to generate a new key)

The key is saved by default in the `.keystore` file in the directory in which you ran this command.

Now, we need to export the certificate from the keystore. We will need the certificate to create the truststore. To export the certificate, run the following command:

```
$ keytool -export -alias mykey -keystore .keystore -rfc -file
certificate.cer
Enter keystore password:
Certificate stored in file <certificate.cer>
```

You were asked about the password to the keystore (the one that you noted down in the previous step), and the certificate was stored in the `certificate.cer` file.

Now, here's the last step: let's create the truststore. Run the following command. You will be asked for the keystore's password and to confirm (by writing `yes`) that you want to trust the given certificate:

```
$ keytool -import -alias mykey -file certificate.cer -keystore
.truststore
Enter keystore password:
```

```
Re-enter new password:

Owner: CN=John Smith, OU=IT Department, O=ACME Corporation, L=Warsaw,
ST=mazowieckie, C=PL

Issuer: CN=John Smith, OU=IT Department, O=ACME Corporation, L=Warsaw,
ST=mazowieckie, C=PL

Serial number: 59a9be54

Valid from: Tue Nov 17 21:40:49 CET 2015 until: Wed Nov 16 21:40:49 CET
2016
Certificate fingerprints:
    MD5:   6F:58:7B:89:13:BB:52:75:33:C6:09:78:91:CD:33:89

    SHA1: F9:DE:D5:BB:29:50:9E:8F:05:20:C6:7F:9D:F5:13:5F:2D:EA:61:00

    SHA256: 55:2E:2A:31:07:08:06:23:F8:42:43:3F:C0:E7:FB:6C:07:38:CD:AB:02
:5C:28:BC:49:87:E3:6E:2B:38:05:AD

    Signature algorithm name: SHA256withRSA

    Version: 3


Extensions:


#1: ObjectId: 2.5.29.14 Criticality=false
SubjectKeyIdentifier [
KeyIdentifier [
0000: 18 78 04 47 98 6B 68 4F   22 33 E4 F0 C0 AF CF B5   .x.G.khO"3......
0010: 76 0A 01 82                                         v...
]
]


Trust this certificate? [no]:  yes
Certificate was added to keystore
```

If you did everything properly, the information would be saved to the
`.truststore` file.

At any time, you can check your keystores using the following command; after you
provide the store's password, its contents will be listed:

```
$ keytool -list -keystore .truststore
Enter keystore password:


Keystore type: JKS
```

```
Keystore provider: SUN
```

```
Your keystore contains 1 entry
```

```
mykey, 17-Nov-2015, trustedCertEntry,
```

Certificate fingerprint (SHA1): F9:DE:D5:BB:29:50:9E:8F:05:20:C6:7F:9D:F5
:13:5F:2D:EA:61:00

Now, let's use these keystores in our code.

Using keystores in the Java code

Let's begin with the server's code. Get the code from the `MyMultiplexedServer.java` file and copy it to `MySecureMultiplexedServer.java`; remember to also update the class name to `MySecureMultiplexedServer`, and add following imports:

```java
import org.apache.thrift.transport.TSSLTransportFactory;
import org.apache.thrift.transport.TSSLTransportFactory.
TSSLTransportParameters;
```

We will be substituting the `myserver` method. Instead of its original content, let's use the following code:

```java
public static void myserver(TMultiplexedProcessor processor) {

    // create parameters store for TSSLTransport
    TSSLTransportParameters params = new
TSSLTransportParameters();

    // point to the keystore, provide keystore's password
    // remember about giving the proper path
    params.setKeyStore(".keystore", "somepassword", null, null);

    // construct the transport, server and start serving
    TServerTransport serverTransport = TSSLTransportFactory.
getServerSocket(8081, 0, null, params);
    TServer server = new TThreadPoolServer(new TThreadPoolServer.
Args(serverTransport).processor(processor));
    System.out.println("Starting secure multiplexed server on port
8081...");
    server.serve();
    }
```

To serve our service over a secure connection, we need to provide the path to our keystore file and the password. It will be run on port 8081 of the localhost.

Now, let's get to the client; you need to perform very similar work to the one you did for the server. First, get the code from the `MyMultiplexedClient.java` file and copy it to `MySecureMultiplexedClient.java`; remember to also update the class name to `MySecureMultiplexedClient`. Then, add the imports:

```
import org.apache.thrift.transport.TSSLTransportFactory;
import org.apache.thrift.transport.TSSLTransportFactory.
TSSLTransportParameters;
```

We will be substituting the following — not secure — part of the code:

```
TTransport transport = new TSocket("localhost", 8080);
transport.open();
```

Instead, we will use the code that will let us connect to the secure server running on port `8081`:

```
TSSLTransportParameters params = new
TSSLTransportParameters();

// point to the keystore, provide keystore's password
// remember about giving the proper path
params.setTrustStore(".truststore", "somepassword");

// construct the transport
transport = TSSLTransportFactory.getClientSocket("localhost",
8081, 0, params);
```

Note that in this case, there's no need to use `transport.open()` as this function is called by the transport method.

Now you have everything that you need to run the secure server and client.

Real-world examples of the usage of Apache Thrift

Up to this point, you learned lots of theoretical details about Apache Thrift and did the development on your own. You know its capabilities and limitations, and I hope you know that it is a great tool to use with many applications. However, is this tool really something that is used in real life?

In this section, I will show you how some well-known, worldwide companies that use Apache Thrift in their operations. You will learn about how it is applied in Facebook, Evernote, Twitter, and some other popular services.

FBThrift in Facebook

Facebook (http://www.facebook.com/) is a company that needs no introduction. With 1.49 billion active users every month, it is used by roughly 20% of the Earth's population. As you know from *Chapter 1, Introducing Apache Thrift*, Facebook engineers are the original authors of the framework. They developed it in 2006 and used it as an internal tool to provide application intercommunication. A year later, they decided to open source it and pass it to the Apache Foundation.

So, do they still develop and use it or has it become obsolete? The truth is that there has never been a better time for Thrift in Facebook. A recent article on the company's developer blog (https://code.facebook.com/posts/1468950976659943/) sheds some light on what's going on.

The framework is used in more than 100 production services implemented mostly in C++, Java, PHP, and Python. It is being actively developed and tweaked by their engineers. One of the most remarkable examples is the Messenger mobile application, which uses Thrift to transmit messages between the server and client.

Technically, in Facebook, it is not Apache Thrift. They started their own fork (separate version) of the software and called it **FBThrift**. It is open source too and is available as a repository on GitHub at https://github.com/facebook/fbthrift. This code is independently maintained, but both its authors and Apache Thrift contributors hope to merge it with the original branch. You may want to consider using this version if your needs are similar to those of Facebook.

FBThrift's idea is to upgrade Apache Thrift to provide higher performance and support for complex features. Over time, Facebook's services evolved from the simplest ones to being increasingly complex, with some services calling other services and its latency or memory footprint started to be an issue.

They worked to improve performance, mainly by implementing parallel processing. They also updated the code to use Folly (https://github.com/facebook/folly), Facebook's open source C++ library of components designed keeping performance in mind.

The other need was to provide more complex features needed by their services. The C++ compiler is completely rewritten and available as the cpp2 generator in the FBThrift codebase. Tests indicate that the services moved to the code generated by it showed significantly better performance: latency decreased by up to 50% and there's a much smaller memory footprint.

As FBThrift is the foundation of Facebook's systems architecture, we may expect lots of further improvements in the future.

If you are interested in trying out FBThrift, check out its GitHub page. You will find detailed installation instructions for several popular platforms (CentOS, Ubuntu 12.04, and 14.04).

Apache Thrift in Evernote

Evernote (`http://www.evernote.com/`) is a popular cross-platform service, designed to take notes and organize information. Its applications are present on all major operating systems and mobile devices. Since its start in 2008, it's gained significant popularity with over 11 million users.

The leading feature of the service is its ability to work on one's notes stored in the cloud using different devices or web applications. In the company CTO's article on Evernote Tech Blog (`https://blog.evernote.com/tech/2011/05/26/evernote-and-thrift/`), we can read some information about the internal process behind choosing Apache Thrift as the best solution for their needs. It is a great insight into what to take into consideration when looking for the most suitable framework for your service.

Evernote's engineers wanted to design a universal API that will serve both thin clients (web browsers, which only serve fragments of the dataset as needed) and thick ones (applications that synchronize the whole user's database at once). They had some requirements that weren't easy to match. First of all, they wanted their API to be cross-platform (they had code in a few different languages, such as Java, C++, and Objective-C), and they wanted to have native bindings for each of them. Another important thing was binary efficiency. As the notes might contain binary attachment, there shouldn't be much overhead (that is, when binary data is encoded using the Base64 encoding, the overhead is 33%, so a 20 MB file is transmitted as a 27 MB payload). Moreover, another important issue was to offer backward compatibility. So, even users using the old version of the software will be able to connect and work with the API. The last two requirements were that the framework should be open source and not too big in terms of code complexity.

They spent a significant amount of time reviewing and testing different options, including some of those that we discussed in *Chapter 1, Introducing Apache Thrift*. When they tested Apache Thrift, they noticed that it fulfills all of their requirements, especially those that are important when building an external API for applications installed on end users' machines: backward compatibility and efficiency in transferring binary data.

As a result, the Evernote Service API (`https://dev.evernote.com/doc/`) was developed using Apache Thrift. It is an open API that allows developers to build their own applications and there are lots of them. You can check them at `https://appcenter.evernote.com/`. The documentation provides good tutorials and code examples, so you can try working with their APIs on your own.

What makes Evernote's usage of Apache Thrift different from Facebook's (and other popular use cases), is that they use it to expose not internal, but public services. This poses more challenges in terms of security, performance, and compatibility. You learned in the previous section of this chapter how to deal with such issues.

Apache Thrift in Twitter

Twitter (`http://www.twitter.com/`) is another extremely popular company that uses Apache Thrift to power many of its internal services. What is interesting and useful for developers is that this company releases lots of the tools that they create as open source, for everyone to use. Here, I will highlight some of the most interesting ones.

Finagle (`http://twitter.github.io/finagle/`) is one of the most interesting of Twitter's projects. It is a protocol-agnostic, asynchronous RPC system for the JVM (so it can be used for Java, Scala, Clojure, Groovy, and others). It may be considered as an extra level of abstraction above Apache Thrift services because it integrates services using different protocols (not only Thrift, but also MySQL, Mux, HTTP, and so on). You may consider researching this solution if you have some services already in place and would like to integrate them with your new Apache Thrift services. Finagle is actively developed and used in production not only by Twitter itself, but also by well-known companies, such as Foursquare, ING Bank, The New York Times, Pinterest, and Tumblr. You may read about some case studies on the Adopters page at `https://github.com/twitter/finagle/blob/master/ADOPTERS.md`.

Scrooge (`https://github.com/twitter/scrooge`) is a replacement for the original Apache Thrift code generator for Scala and Java, which is recommended for use with Finagle.

Diffy (`https://github.com/twitter/diffy`) is another great tool from Twitter, useful for everyone writing Apache Thrift and HTTP-based services. The purpose of this tool is to test different versions of the same service, find the differences in them, evaluate the problems that may occur, or help fix bugs. The idea is simple: the old stable (`primary`) and new (`candidate`) services are run side by side, and every request sent to Diffy, which acts as a proxy, is passed on to them. Then, the results are compared and potential differences are detected and reported in the form of a nice report. Diffy uses a nice trick to filter out some nondeterministic noises (such as some random results, timestamps, and so on) by sending the payload to the third instance (`secondary`) for comparison. This tool allows performing tests and development a lot quicker compared to writing traditional integration tests. You will need the **Scala Build Tool** (**SBT**), which you can download from `http://www.scala-sbt.org/`, to run Diffy.

There are some more Apache Thrift-related tools that you can check out on Twitter. If you wish to start using their toolbox, I suggest browsing their GitHub profile (https://github.com/twitter) for yourself and taking your pick.

Apache Thrift in other companies

Apache Thrift is a popular solution among top companies. However, as it is used mainly internally, information on this is rarely public. However, many companies, Twitter and Facebook being notable examples, share their knowledge and the tools that they develop internally so that we can learn a little bit more about their internals and Apache Thrift usage.

Pinterest (https://www.pinterest.com/) is one such enterprise. It runs a website and mobile applications that let users upload, organize, and share photos. It uses Apache Thrift internally, though not much information on this is available. However, it does share useful tools; one of them is the thrift-tools application and library, available at https://github.com/pinterest/thrift-tools. It is a great debugging appliance as it allows you to observe the requests coming to your service and the resulting responses. Let's look at this example from the documentation:

```
$ sudo thrift-tool --iface eth0 --port 9091 dump --show-all -pretty
[00:39:42:850848] 10.1.8.7:49858 -> 10.1.2.20:3636: method=dosomething,
type=call, seqid=1120
header: ()
fields: [    (    'struct',
         1,
         [    ('string', 1, 'something to do'),
             ('i32', 3, 0),
             (    'struct',
                 9,
                 [    ('i32', 3, 2),
                     ('i32', 14, 0),
                     ('i32', 16, 0),
                     ('i32', 18, 25)])])]
------>[00:39:42:856204] 10.1.2.20:3636 -> 10.1.8.7:49858:
method=dosomething, type=reply, seqid=1120
         header: ()
         fields: [    (    'struct',
         0,
```

```
[    ('string', 1, 'did something'),
     ('string', 2, 'did something else'),
     ('string', 3, 'did some other thing'),
     ('string', 4, 'did the last thing'),
     ('i32', 6, 3),
     ('i32', 7, 11),
     ('i32', 8, 0),
     ('i32', 9, 0),
     ('list', 10, [0]),
```

Note that it requires elevated privileges and uses low-level network tools, so it may or may not work in your environment.

Another interesting tool from Pinterest is the `quasar-thrift` library (`https://github.com/pinterest/quasar-thrift`), which integrates Apache Thrift with Quasar (`http://docs.paralleluniverse.co/quasar/`), the library that provides high-performance, lightweight threads for JVM languages. This library provides a high-performance server that's fully compatible with Apache Thrift. You may want to consider it if you need highly-performing services in the JVM environment.

Flipkart (`http://www.flipkart.com/`) is one of the biggest e-commerce businesses in India with 8 million orders monthly and 10 million page views per day. According to a presentation by Siddhartha Reddy, Tech Lead is in charge of search and browse experience at Flipkart (`http://www.slideshare.net/sids/how-flipkart-scales-php`). It uses the Apache Thrift binary services to support scalability of its PHP applications.

Phantom (`https://github.com/Flipkart/phantom`) is a tool similar to Twitter's Finagle; it is a high-performance proxy for the accessing of distributed services. It supports not only Apache Thrift but also HTTP, MySQL, and Avro and lets you write your own protocol proxies. You may want to consider it when integrating your Apache Thrift services in an environment where other services are already present.

There are many more well-known companies using Apache Thrift, including Uber, Siemens, Last.fm, and reCAPTCHA. You may check the official lists at `https://thrift.apache.org/about` and `https://wiki.apache.org/thrift/PoweredBy`. I hope that after reading this book, you will be able to use Apache Thrift in your application on a significant scale; don't forget to add in your company's name too!

Summary

In this chapter, you learned a lot about what to think of while designing Apache Thrift services that will be deployed to the production environment. We discussed not only Apache Thrift's capabilities, but also some extra tools that are essential in every project, no matter the technology.

We mentioned the performance techniques such as multiplexing, and discussed the choice of the best server. You should also know how to secure your service using SSL/TLS.

To show you a better view of the Apache Thrift community, we also covered how this great piece of software is developed and maintained in the biggest companies in the world.

Now that you've managed to go through all of the examples in each chapter, I must congratulate you and pat you on the back for being a great learner. I'm sure I managed to interest you in the topic of Apache Thrift, and you will reach for this book again when developing your own services.

Through this book, you learned about the technical details of Apache Thrift, its internals, and how to use it in your project. Finally, you got some extra information that I hope will inspire you to look at further possibilities for expanding your knowledge about Apache Thrift and its related subjects.

Let's move to a new beginning of development using Apache Thrift, which is a great piece of software. It stays in the shadows, but powers lots of the services that we consider staples of the modern Internet. The documentation on it is sparse, and you need to persevere and perform some tests to achieve the result you need, but in the end, you get this powerful tool that works like a charm.

When you work on your tools or provide improvements to Apache Thrift, consider contributing them to the open source community for the benefit of all your fellow developers.

If you would like to express your opinion about the book or share your Apache Thrift story, don't hesitate to contact me at `krzysztof@rakowski.pro`.

Index

Thank you for buying
Learning Apache Thrift

About Packt Publishing

Packt, pronounced 'packed', published its first book, *Mastering phpMyAdmin for Effective MySQL Management*, in April 2004, and subsequently continued to specialize in publishing highly focused books on specific technologies and solutions.

Our books and publications share the experiences of your fellow IT professionals in adapting and customizing today's systems, applications, and frameworks. Our solution-based books give you the knowledge and power to customize the software and technologies you're using to get the job done. Packt books are more specific and less general than the IT books you have seen in the past. Our unique business model allows us to bring you more focused information, giving you more of what you need to know, and less of what you don't.

Packt is a modern yet unique publishing company that focuses on producing quality, cutting-edge books for communities of developers, administrators, and newbies alike. For more information, please visit our website at www.packtpub.com.

About Packt Open Source

In 2010, Packt launched two new brands, Packt Open Source and Packt Enterprise, in order to continue its focus on specialization. This book is part of the Packt Open Source brand, home to books published on software built around open source licenses, and offering information to anybody from advanced developers to budding web designers. The Open Source brand also runs Packt's Open Source Royalty Scheme, by which Packt gives a royalty to each open source project about whose software a book is sold.

Writing for Packt

We welcome all inquiries from people who are interested in authoring. Book proposals should be sent to author@packtpub.com. If your book idea is still at an early stage and you would like to discuss it first before writing a formal book proposal, then please contact us; one of our commissioning editors will get in touch with you.

We're not just looking for published authors; if you have strong technical skills but no writing experience, our experienced editors can help you develop a writing career, or simply get some additional reward for your expertise.

Learning Firefox OS Application Development

ISBN: 978-1-78398-940-9   Paperback: 166 pages

Learn to design, build, and deploy your Firefox OS applications, built with web technologies, to the Firefox Marketplace

1. Create beautiful and interactive Firefox OS applications by applying your knowledge of web development.

2. Cater your applications to a huge number of users by porting them to the Firefox OS.

3. A step-by-step learning workflow with real-life applications to demonstrate the concepts.

Apache Maven Cookbook

ISBN: 978-1-78528-612-4   Paperback: 272 pages

Over 90 hands-on recipes to successfully build and automate development life cycle tasks following Maven conventions and best practices

1. Understand the features of Apache Maven that makes it a powerful tool for build automation.

2. Full of real-world scenarios covering multi-module builds and best practices to make the most out of Maven projects.

3. A step-by-step tutorial guide full of pragmatic examples.

Please check **www.PacktPub.com** for information on our titles

open source *
community experience distilled

Apache Flume: Distributed
Log Collection for Hadoop
Second Edition

Design and implement a series of Flume agents to send streamed
data into Hadoop

Steve Hoffman

[PACKT] open source *

Apache Flume: Distributed Log Collection for Hadoop
Second Edition

ISBN: 978-1-78439-217-8   Paperback: 178 pages

Design and implement a series of Flume agents to
send streamed data into Hadoop

1. Construct a series of Flume agents using
   the Apache Flume service to efficiently
   collect, aggregate, and move large amounts
   of event data.

2. Configure failover paths and load balancing to
   remove single points of failure.

3. Use this step-by-step guide to stream logs from
   application servers to Hadoop's HDFS.

**Getting Started with
Apache Maven**

Russell Gold

[PACKT] VIDEO

Getting Started with Apache Maven [Video]

ISBN: 978-1-78216-572-9   Duration: 02:15 hrs

Design and manage simple to complex Java projects
effectively using Apache Maven's project object model

1. Covers everything from basic dependencies to
   complex multi-module projects.

2. Demonstrates the key concept of project
   building logically.

3. Loaded with examples, motivated by typical
   build challenges.

Please check **www.PacktPub.com** for information on our titles